CERI RICHARDS

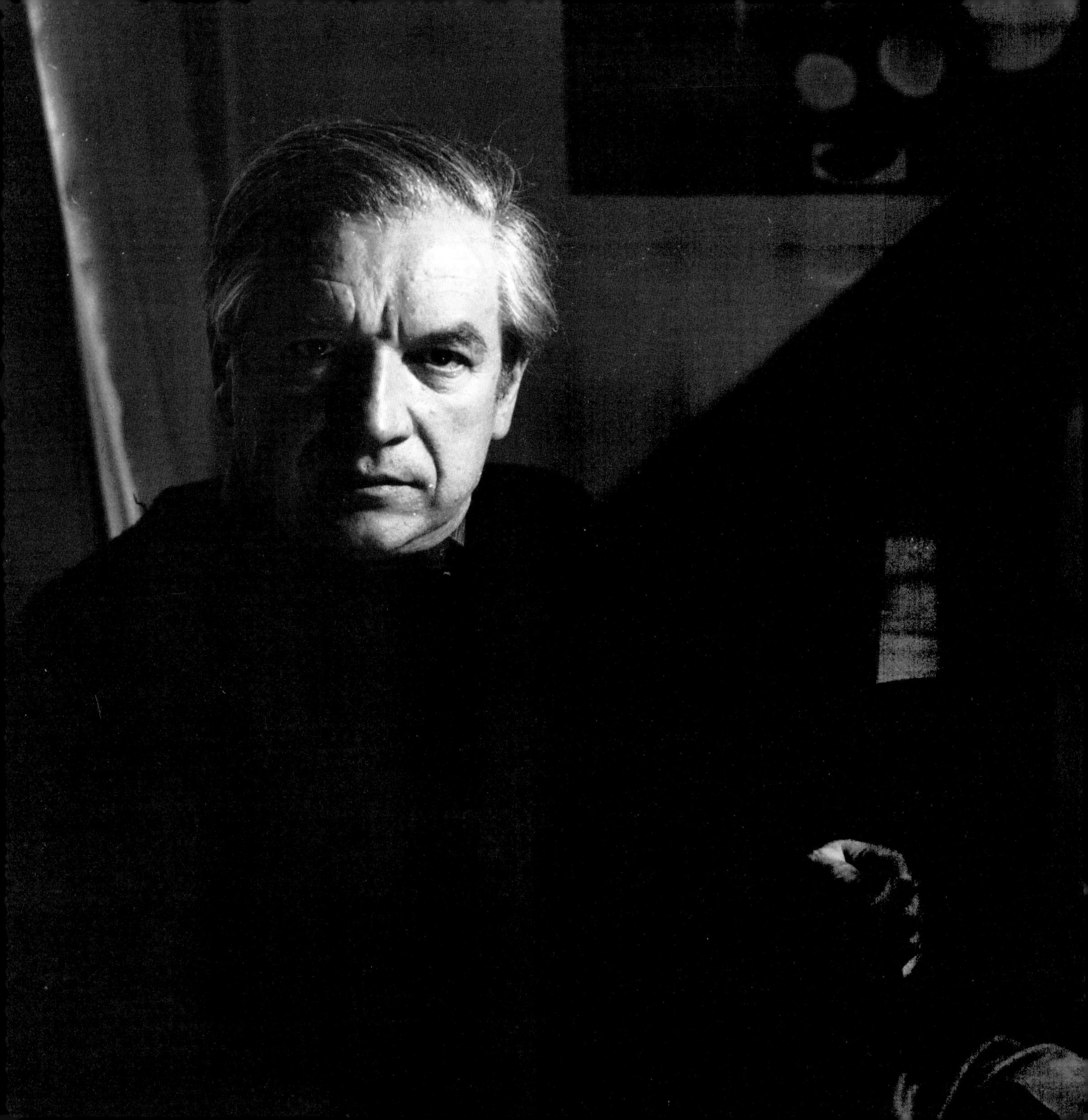

CERI RICHARDS

THE TATE GALLERY

ISBN 0 905005 13 9
Published by order of the Trustees 1981
for the exhibition of 22 July – 6 September 1981
Copyright © 1981 The Tate Gallery
Published by the Tate Gallery Publications Department
Millbank, London SW1P 4RG
Designed by Caroline Johnston
Printed in Great Britain by Balding + Mansell, Wisbech, Cambs.

Contents

cover
94 Harvest 1969

frontispiece
Ceri Richards, Chelsea, 1968

Foreword

Ceri Richards served the Tate Gallery as a Trustee for many years, and we are happy to remember him with this retrospective exhibition. He was a most unusual artist, gifted with a fine poetic imagination and an innate love of fantasy that few of his contemporaries possessed. He drew with ease and naturalness and had a marvellous ability to make the arresting image.

As a young artist in the thirties he had shown with the surrealists, and the constructions that he made at this time are amongst his most original works. Like so many of his generation his natural development as an artist was grievously interrupted by the war. Later he seemed always to stand apart, he was very much an individual who preferred to go his own way. His response to music and poetry was unusually profound, and often dictated his choice of subject matter. He was an admirer of the Welsh poets, Vernon Watkins and Dylan Thomas, both Swansea-born like himself, and lines of their verse could inspire him as readily and totally as the sight of tourists in Trafalgar Square, or the hospital patient in the opposite bed.

Music was however his greatest love, and it was in the piano Preludes of Debussy that he discovered subjects that awoke the full flight of his imagination. To hear him play this music was an especial delight, for Ceri was a natural musician of a remarkable order. But then he was altogether a man of great integrity, modesty and generosity, and those who knew him personally remember him with affection and gratitude.

We were fortunate in persuading Bryan Robertson to select the exhibition and write the illuminating catalogue introduction that follows. It was in 1960 that he arranged at the Whitechapel Art Gallery what was certainly the most important exhibition that Ceri Richards ever had, and one that confirmed his status as a major figure. Mr Robertson has been greatly helped in the selection of work by the artist's widow, Mrs Frances Richards, and by Mel Gooding, who has also compiled the biographical material in the catalogue.

The artist's family has lent generously to the exhibition, and to them and to the many lenders, both public and private, we are most grateful. Their names appear on page 72.

After the Tate Gallery the exhibition will be shown in Swansea, at the Glynn Vivian Art Gallery from 3 October to 7 November, as part of the Swansea Festival of Music and the Arts. No second venue could be more appropriate for a Ceri Richards exhibition, and we at the Tate Gallery are delighted to know that his fellow countrymen will have the opportunity of seeing the work of this great Welshman.

Alan Bowness, *Director*

Introduction

I The Character of the Artist

Ceri Richards seemed always to live entirely within his work or to exist self-sufficiently behind the protective shield of his family. I was first stirred and elated by his paintings of pianists in interiors in the late nineteen forties and the cheerful Trafalgar Square series of paintings in 1951, painted to celebrate the Festival of Britain. Ceri was already middle-aged when I first met him a year or two later in the early nineteen fifties, a man of medium height, thick-set but not flabby, rather powerfully built and with a strong, oddly restrained but alert and listening presence as if he were considering something, some factor, outside and beyond the boundaries of the conversation. He was a distinguished and good-looking man, rather like a more conventionally handsome Picasso and, apart from his greying hair, he did not seem to change much over the years. With this curiously intent presence, at once watchful and withdrawn, there came also a strong impression of a fundamentally innocent man: not silly by any means and even quite reasonably worldly-wise, but still a man without the usual barriers of artifice or self-preservation.

Because Ceri seemed always so defenceless against what he still considered the basic Philistinism of the British public in the fifties or the vagaries of fashion that were so impossible for a serious artist to deal with, he aroused a protective streak in me. He had been unalterably conditioned by the near-impossibility of finding a receptive audience for abstract or, more properly, his own semi-abstract art in the nineteen thirties when Ceri, as a young man, began to find his form. I felt that I should try to help this vulnerable man, with such formidable gifts that were not always clearly recognised beyond a comparatively small circle of admirers, but of course all that I could do was to write about his work with enthusiasm a couple of times and, more usefully perhaps, prepare the first retrospective exhibition of his work to be seen in London at Whitechapel in 1960. This exhibition was a considerable success and marked the beginning of a generally more expansive phase in Ceri's career: he signed a contract with the Marlborough Gallery at that time, which must have held out the possibility that his work would be exhibited abroad, and he was selected to represent England at the Venice Biennale in 1962.

I should add that my feelings of admiration, and concern for Ceri's full recognition, have been fully shared by three successive Directors of the Tate Gallery: by Sir Norman Reid who succeeded Sir John Rothenstein and was Director until 1980, and by Alan Bowness, the Tate's present Director, who initiated the present exhibition. Alan Bowness was writing with enthusiasm about Ceri's work twenty years ago in the press, and so, it should be said, were Patrick Heron, John Berger, Roberto Sanesi, Robert Melville, Michael Levey and John Russell. David Thompson wrote a deeply considered essay for the catalogue accompanying the Ceri Richards exhibition at Whitechapel in 1960, and was the author of a short monograph on Richards in 1963. Other notable supporters of Richards in written criticism include John Ormond, the Welsh poet, who also made a film about the artist in 1968. An earlier film about Richards was made in 1963 by Dudley Shaw Ashton. In 1975, Alan Bowness organised for the Edinburgh Festival the first large gathering of the artist's work, concentrating on musical and poetic connections, since his memorial show in Wales in 1973. This unusually broad and committed range of critical support was matched on several occasions by the patronage of Sir Colin Anderson, a distinguished collector of British art with much charm and understanding of artists who, as Chairman of the Orient Line, was also able to commission Ceri, in the economically depressed year of 1935, to design a collage for SS *Orion*. But critical support, although useful, is only words on paper and not always instrumental in selling paintings. Colin Anderson's occasional patronage could not secure Ceri from the usual pressures of teaching and the customary economic stringencies from which the artist was not really free until the last decade of his life. It is true to say that his work is held in high esteem by informed opinion everywhere, and with special warmth by fellow artists, but he did not achieve the broad popularity of Henry Moore or even Sutherland, although in my view his work should be considered at the same level of radical achievement in British art as the sculptures of Moore and Hepworth or the paintings of Sutherland, Nicholson, Hitchens and Bacon.

We must have met and talked, Ceri and myself, many times during the preparations for the 1960 Whitechapel show, but I have no memory of any particularly sharp or idiosyncratic views on art or on anything else for that matter, and his surviving friends confirm this impression. He was a private man, who restricted his conversation mostly to the work in hand, or to fairly conventional expressions of approval or sympathy for the work of certain artists, composers or poets, some of whose music and poems played a considerable part in his thoughts as the direct or oblique inspiration for his own work. In speaking of art, music or literature, Ceri's soft Welsh voice took on the warm tones of enthusiasm, the sort of enthusiasm when considering something peerless and beyond all normal achievement, that you more usually find in the accents of much younger men. He always spoke of art and artists with respect and he kept an old fashioned and extremely likeable sense of professional camaraderie. He did not envy success in others but was instead pleased to see any signs of advancement in the public or individual acceptance of modern art.

As Henry Moore has said, in a written tribute (in the catalogue for Homage to C.R. exhibition, Fischer Fine Art, 1972), 'Ceri never spoke badly of anyone.' The most critical verdict that I ever heard him give of any painting, poem or piece of music was that he did not understand it or that the work in question was not really for him. He was at all times gentle and courteous in his manner and he found an equivalent for this in the unaffectedly respectful but warm way in which he discussed all forms of art.

Living so much inside his family, with his wife Frances and his daughters, Rachel and Rhiannon, it seems that Ceri did not really have a particularly close male friend, other than the several artists who, with their wives, formed a loose circle of friends from the thirties on, with very little change. These friends included the sculptor F.E. McWilliam and his wife Beth, Mary Fedden and Julian Trevelyan, Margerie and Merlyn Evans and Robert Medley and Rupert Doone. Francis Bacon was also a friend and warm admirer of Ceri's work. Henry Moore was a supporter of Ceri from student days onward, and owns a major painting. But Ceri had no specially close crony for the intimate exchange of views on art or life and, although he appreciated good food and drink, he could never have been said to have been a drinking man: he had no interest in the sociable fraternity of pubs or bars. Although he seemed to enjoy parties, he retained always a certain smiling and amiable reserve.

He was in fact rather a shy man, and he always kept about him the sense of being an expatriate from another country, which of course he was, somewhat ill at ease in the sophistications of London, and happiest inside the reassuring intimacies of family life which continued the happy domestic framework of his childhood and boyhood years in Wales: a typically Welsh pattern. This faint but very real air of a retiring country cousin puzzled me. It was difficult to avoid feeling that as Ceri had such an instinctively refined and shaped imagination, at ease, as it were, in the symbolist legacy of Mallarmé, Yeats or Redon as if he had been born with innate knowledge of poetic and visual metaphor, sign and symbol, and with an equally direct feeling for the abstract and surrealist language of art in the nineteen thirties which so perfectly caught and extended his own sense of form, it was misplaced modesty and reticence on his part to assume that others were so much more sophisticated or better educated, formally, than himself.

He was certainly at home, from his earliest years, with the newest developments in the visual language of his time. In addition, his taste in music was quite sufficiently advanced even in his youth to be aroused by the music of Webern, Berg and Schönberg, as well as by later developments in music, and he read widely, with always a special preference for poetry. It was sometimes hard to reconcile all this with the diffidence of a provincial, not quite at home in the sophisticated city, but on Ceri's part, I know, the diffidence was quite unaffected.

Everyone who knew him agreed that despite the friendly amiability of his manner, Ceri did not commit himself to any memorable utterances or even extreme opinions in his conversation. He gave out a feeling of moderation in all things and yet he transmitted, too, an odd expectancy in those he met for some extra-ordinary communication, serious or frivolous, which was never divulged. For as a parallel to his odd way of combining reticence or a withdrawn elusiveness with an alert and listening presence, Ceri also managed often to convey a slightly excited and amused manner that promised scandalous or at least very sharp disclosures which were, in the event, never forthcoming. This air of imminent revelation of some either funny or dramatic item of news or information, sometimes accompanied by a simple question, would flare up every now and then, usually on first meeting after an absence of communication for a few weeks, but nothing was ever forthcoming and Ceri would soon subside into his usual friendly placidity.

Writing with special perception in 1973, his fellow Welshman, the poet John Ormond, said in the catalogue for the Ceri Richards Memorial Exhibition at the National Museum of Wales: 'He talked in little bursts, with a soft voice, his words darting, minute facets between phrases, never at a loss for a word but naturally quiet and, in company, slightly hesitant in manner. Important matters he seemed sure about without being self-righteous or ponderous. But small things he seemed to note with a surprise that would widen into a smile. He was a compassionate man.'

He was almost certainly more at ease talking to fellow artists than anyone else, being free of any sense of rivalry with other artists and, although he served conscientiously as a Trustee of the Tate Gallery from 1958–1965, the meetings with their difficult judge-ments and decisions must have been often un-congenial to him.

In a recent note to me, the sculptor F.E. McWilliam, an old friend of the artist who owns two of his best paintings has said: 'Ceri had absolutely no interest in art politics, he never saw art as being *competitive*. The only things which stopped him painting were when he had to teach and his Trustee meetings at the Tate – these upset him so much that he always armed himself beforehand with a tranquiliser, then worried afterwards in case he had agreed to something he should have objected to.'

But in trying to establish Ceri's singularly quiet and unaggressive personality, it is easy to conceal the strong charm of the man inadvertently in a shroud of virtue and blandness. So it is also true to say that Ceri often radiated a strong sense of fun and enjoyment of life. McWilliam remembers an unexpected dry note in Ceri's otherwise equable reactions to the comments of others. According to McWilliam, Ceri was on friendly terms over some years with a doctor who painted in his spare time and who one day regaled Ceri with a long account of the trouble that he had been through in handling a particular colour. He finished a lengthy account of his struggles with art by telling the bemused Ceri that he, too, should have a spare-time hobby, as the doctor had chosen painting to serve as a refreshing refuge from the familiar problems of the working day. McWilliam asked Ceri if he had reminded his doctor friend of his own musical life and the hours he spent in playing the piano. 'No', said Ceri, 'I told him I was thinking of becoming a Sunday gynaecologist.'

Julian Trevelyan also recalls asking Ceri if a drawing in his possession of a tightly packed bevy of female nudes disporting themselves across the page was really the traditional subject of Cleopatra's Barge. 'Oh no', Ceri said, 'it's a brothel in a Welsh mining valley.'

The peace and security that Ceri enjoyed inside his own family was not a simple matter of domestic routine and the passive pleasures of everyday living. He worked long hours in his studio, even in the earlier years when he was teaching, so that time spent with his wife and daughters was precious for him. And as there had been in his family life as a child, there was always within his marriage a cultivated love of music as well as literature and art in general.

Ceri's sister, Esther, ten years younger than her brother (another brother, Owen, was also on close terms with Ceri but died in 1980), has described to me the way in which music, literature and art played such a vigorous and unselfconscious part in the daily family life of Ceri's early years so that, although the monetary resources of the family were modest, when Ceri eventually took the decision to study to be a professional artist, there were no warning notes or any real surprise from the family, only pleasure and every effort to help. The decision seemed quite natural to everyone, even in the stringent economic circumstances of the early and mid twenties.

Mel Gooding has compiled a biographical chronology of the artist's life (see page 22) which describes also his parentage and early years in Dunvant, a village near Swansea, in Glamorganshire, but a number of observations made to me by Ceri's sister, Esther, not only describe the family scene in her youth but also provide useful insights into Ceri's development. First, Esther remembers walking regularly with Ceri when he was about eighteen years old, to Clyne Common, near Swansea, and waiting for long periods while Ceri made watercolour paintings of the trees and scrubby landscape around them. Of more direct influence in Ceri's later development was the coastline: the cliffs, rocks, rockpools, sea and beaches of the surrounding Gower peninsula. At this time, Ceri had no clear thought of becoming a professional artist, but he explored at length and assiduously this stretch of coast.

In addition, Ceri as a boy made innumerable drawn decorations in the preliminary or end papers of books, a practice which he was to continue in later years when, in addition to separate drawings and paintings which were stimulated by certain poems, Ceri also made coloured drawings on the page around individual poems printed in books of poems by Dylan Thomas and Vernon Watkins. I believe that the printed words containing the meaning of certain lines of poetry had as much excitement for Ceri as the evocative chords and harmonies in particular pieces of music and in this sense the printed page with its white margins and spaces would act as a magnetic field for the artist's own calligraphy and decorative flair, aroused by his sense of the poem's inner meaning.

The character of these embellishments changed, of course, from the comparatively simple decorations of his boyhood to the more complex imagery of his maturity but the passion for extending the life of a poem in this way persisted all his life. Before embarking in *c.*1945 on the painting inspired by the poem *c.*1934 of Dylan Thomas, 'The force that through the green fuse drives the flower' (drawing no. I), Ceri felt impelled to write out the poem in his own handwriting in pen and ink, which he then embellished most elaborately with the images of growth, seeding and fruitfulness, with their intertwined metamorphoses into human references, which crystallised in the subsequent paintings.

It was as if the artist had to be physically identified with the actual unfolding of the poem as a series of

poetic images and their abstract identification as
letters and words, and I make this reference only to
indicate that poetry for Ceri, like music, was no mere
pretext for superficial decoration but a living, imaginative world to be penetrated, felt and totally assimi-
lated by the artist. Ceri sought always for the image
beyond the words and never their illustration, however
apt or sympathetic; and when, later, he was inspired
by music to make paintings and drawings he was as
aware of the spaces and silences between chords, with
their own architectonic structure, as he was immersed
in melody, rhythm and the dynamics of counterpoint.
And just as the painted letters and words of a poem
moved him, so was he affected in music by the visual
appearance of a keyboard, a stringed instrument or a
printed page of musical notation, just as much as the
music itself. These images had great potency for him
and appear in much of his work.

Ceri's sister, Esther, has other memories of her
brother's early years which throw light on his later
character as an artist. Although Ceri had no clear idea
of becoming an artist when he attended Gowerton
Grammar School, limiting his activity to the pleasures
of decorating books and making descriptive water-
colours and drawings out of doors, the decision to be a
professional artist was made in 1920 when Ceri was
seventeen, immediately after the failure of the local
electrical engineering firm where he had been briefly
apprenticed after leaving grammar school. He quickly
enrolled as a full-time student at Swansea School of Art.

The decision was warmly supported by many
friends in the village as well as the family, and before
moving on to art school, Ceri had two private tutors to
instruct him in art. This special tuition may not have
been particularly relevant or helpful to Ceri's subsequent work as an art student, but the fact that
special tuition in art was found for him pinpoints the
moment when the decision was taken to become a
professional artist, and emphasises the ready support
Ceri received from his family. The art tuition was
undoubtedly supported by Ceri's mother, who taught

in the village school, but the decision to become an
artist was still particularly courageous not only
because of the depressed economic times everywhere
but also because Ceri had so little visual encouragement from any art around him. It was not until he
was working at Swansea School of Art as a student
that he had the stimulus of seeing the late Monets in
the collection of the Davies sisters at Gregynog (now
in the National Museum of Wales).

Ceri's father, as Mel Gooding records in his chronology, was passionately involved in music-making and
in choral work. Tom Richards conducted three choirs
for the local chapel and each of his three children was
taught to play the piano. But if there were no pictures
on the walls of his home of any interest to Ceri, as a
boy, a tradition of craftsmen existed on both sides of
the family, carpenters on the maternal side, black-
smiths among Ceri's father's antecedents, who
included Huguenots, and Ceri showed always great
pride in a job well done and in technical excellence.
All this informed the technical brilliance and resource-
fulness of his mature work. His sister believes that his
decision to become an artist, as opposed to undirected
pleasure in school art classes, was taken when, at
sixteen, he painted backcloths for amateur theatrical
performances initiated by his father, and this work
just preceded the special tuition in art.

My old surprise at Ceri's diffident manner, when
I first knew him as an artist of acknowledged
distinction, is now to a large extent dispersed by his
sister's recent and quite unrancorous memory of the
way in which people in Wales, at the time of Ceri's
boyhood, were made to feel inferior to the English. Ceri
grew up speaking only Welsh in the family until he
was five, and then at school according to his sister,
'you were smacked if you were heard speaking
Welsh'. The Welshness of being Welsh, together with
the crucial roots of culture and language, were
considered irrelevant to the serious business of
acquiring an education, and a rather subversive form
of self-indulgence. This negative attitude perhaps gave

Ceri a special sense of mission, to succeed and excel when he came to London, held up to the Welsh as a great citadel of sophistication and power, in 1924 on a scholarship to study at the Royal College of Art, but it was also something to overcome. In later years he was irritated or at least bored if he was too insistently referred to as a 'Welsh artist', as if it were a limitation.

This feeling of expatriate separateness, as well as the sudden expansion of all horizons with attendant challenges and pleasures which the move from a Welsh village to London must have entailed, largely explains the continuation of close family links after Ceri had enrolled at the Royal College of Art, as well as his persistent shyness in later years.

In London, Ceri continued to explore music by attending concerts, as well as by playing the piano. He also played the organ regularly in a Catholic church in Fulham Palace Road. He corresponded with his parents and brother and sister regularly; listened a good deal to preachers in London, including Donald Soper and Dr Maude Royden, and discussed religion in many letters to his father who, in addition to his music making and a love of poetry which he could share with his son, was always interested in theology. He sent his laundry home every week from the college, and in addition to constant letters also received from home a weekly parcel containing food and various small comforts which might also contain runner beans and lilies of the valley, as well as a cake. Ceri's elder daughter, Rachel, born in 1932, remembers parcels of this most basic and affectionate kind arriving in London quite regularly from Wales when she was a child in the thirties, an economically gloomy time when parcels from Wales must have been a cheerful sight.

All through the years of life in London and his own marriage, and the upbringing of his own family, Ceri never lost his intimacy with his father and mother and his brother and sister, continuing to play Mozart and Schubert duets with Esther, on frequent visits to Wales, and arguing and talking with his father who always embraced and kissed Ceri on greeting him, even as a young man. I refer to all these trivial intimacies only to show the deep and close relationship with his family which Ceri always enjoyed, to explain to myself, perhaps, why he always seemed to exist only within his work or behind the protective shield of his family, and to set out the factors of existence in a Welsh chapel community, and an unselfconsciously cultured family life in which art as well as music and poetry played a natural part, as the determining, shaping elements in the artist's make-up.

The strongest part of the family shield, after his father, was his wife, Frances. Ceri met Frances Clayton, from Burslem, Stoke-on-Trent, at a Christmas dance at the Royal College of Art in 1928. This has been recorded by John Ormond, in his essay for the Memorial Exhibition in 1973, but it is worth repeating. 'For two years before winning a major scholarship to the college she had earned her living as a designer in a famous china works. As fellow-students she and Ceri had admired each other's work. Now he asked her out – to a concert. Schoenberg conducted his *Gurrelieder*; Delius, wrapped in his rug, was in the audience; Arnold Bennett sat next to the young couple who were married the following year.

'Frances Richards has always been a fine artist in her own right. Her importance to her husband was that for forty years she supported his vision with her enthusiasm, belief, judgement, and her own hard work. In the early days Richards had to pick up what money he could as a church organist; and for many years he and his wife had to teach in art schools, Mrs Richards bringing up their children as well.' As Alan Bowness has recorded in his introductory essay for the Edinburgh Festival Exhibition in 1976, Ceri had also to work in advertising agencies for ten years after he graduated from the Royal College.

A lively talker with an amused sense of the world around her and absolute devotion to her husband's work and needs, Frances Richards not only protected her shy husband in everyday life and society but helped him always with sharp reactions to his work, which he invited her to see at the end of each working day – she has exceptionally sure judgement of her husband's work. Her forthright presence confronts us in several early paintings and in many drawings. With Ceri's absolute inability to promote himself or to further his own interests, Frances had also the task of asking for money when it was due to him from dealers or school authorities and generally keeping the accounts.

If Ceri's character as an artist was undoubtedly nurtured and protected by his family life, it was also formed by the cliffs and estuaries and emphatic horizon lines dividing sea from sky in the Gower peninsular, a sense of the cosmos and nature reinforced by reading theology and poetry, a passion for plants and flowers and all the signs of vegetable growth gained from looking at the profusion of Welsh country gardens and the surrounding landscape of his youth, a Celtic love for sinuous, flowing contours and glowing colour, and for music which he loved as much as painting. But the final, crucial element in the sources of his inspiration as an artist is, of course, women, love of women, love of their bodies and their fecundity which he saw also as a parallel to the whole regenerative cycle of nature, and of course their erotic complexity.

He had also, rather endearingly, a great affection for the richly burgeoning and alluringly gaudy images of huge flowers, fruits and vegetables on packets of 'Bee's Seeds That Grow' which he used to buy from Woolworths or ironmongers shops in Hammersmith or Chelsea and which he kept by him rather more for the eccentric brilliance of their vision of nature than for any hope for their seeds so extravagantly promised on the packets. These simple images indirectly affected many paintings. The artist mentioned the seed packet illustrations in 1959, when I was looking at paintings in his studio and had told him that one painting in particular looked rather like a magic beanstalk, and Mel Gooding has independently and recently confirmed this background source.

II The Nature of the Work

Before Ceri could use colour effectively, make any comment about life or record any discovery about the world around him, and long before he could make analogies and visual puns about aspects of visual experience which then allowed the character of a metaphor, before he could work with any degree of fluency in any direction, he had to learn to draw. No artist can make eloquent and concise marks on paper or canvas with pencil or brush, to delineate and trap the promptings of either his imagination or subconscious dreamlife without the ability to draw with absolute ease and precision any object, mass, volume, space, form or substance in front of him, in the physical, verifiable world.

Among other things, the practice of drawing is to do with the ease and certainty with which a pencil or a brush is made with absolute directness to make an enlivening and exact mark on paper or canvas. Drawing is not copying. Drawing is a supreme act of visual probity demanding direct coordination between eye, nervous system, imaginative response, and hand and wrist. The pencil or the brush is not unlike the surgeon's scalpel in the act which, for the artist, is not dissection but its reverse, a constructive building up of all the essentially salient aspects of a form: a face, a body, a building, a tree, or an abstract construction. The human body is the strangest, most complicated and beautiful fact of our existence: if you can draw this, you can draw anything, and all artists have known this, from Michelangelo and Rembrandt to Cézanne, Matisse, Picasso and Moore.

The drawings of Ceri Richards are among the finest made in this century, not just by any British artist but among artists anywhere, in Europe or America. There is an unforced ease in the dynamic power of his drawings which can only come from complete mastery over form and its perception as well as through acute discipline over formal ends and technical means. This mastery can only be acquired by practice up to a certain point, beyond that, if the skill is not extended by a profound visual intelligence and a coherent imagination, the drawings turn leaden and become mannered, academic and lifeless. Ceri's drawings are full of life: he virtually could not put a mark on paper without invoking, involuntarily, a suggestive resonance which came from areas of imaginative possibilities far beyond their immediate descriptive task. The ease of these drawings is con-summate and shows the same mastery that Picasso had when he picked up a piece of chalk or even a stick dipped in paint and was able to instantly make a line which was not only the visual apotheosis of a form but also an aesthetic and tactile adventure in itself. Picasso's line turns a mere journey into a voyage. Ceri's drawings also extend the life of their subjects, rather than seal them off, and drawing is the probing, questing, vitalising armature in all his work.

Henry Moore has said of Ceri's draughtsmanship (in the Homage to C.R. catalogue, Fischer Fine Art, 1972), 'What I always admired about Ceri Richards, right from his Royal College of Art student days, was the way he could draw. More than any other British painter of his time he understood three-dimensional form and knew how to express it on a flat surface. His drawing is so assured, so full of energy and virility, that it gives his work a quality that goes way beyond charm. In fact, "charm" isn't the word for it at all: Ceri's work has authority because of his drawing.'

Much earlier, in 1933, John Piper also drew attention to these powers in his drawing: 'In Ceri Richards' drawing there are signs of the quick, excited apprehension of a present experience, a similar fusion with past – perhaps unconscious – experience and a sure statement that only a man well-versed in the mechanics of drawing could make.' This 'quick apprehension fused with past experience' exactly embodies what I mean by 'suggestive resonance beyond descriptive task', and it was because of this suggestive resonance, which extended beyond the immediate completion of a painting, that Ceri so often worked *en serie*.

Ceri's ability to draw had first disclosed itself when he attended evening classes in engineering drawing at Swansea Technical College, when he worked briefly for a firm of electricians before the decision was taken to become an artist and study at art school. By the time he left the Royal College, this basic gift had expanded into a brilliantly expressive ease with line and a precocious command of form. In the early thirties there are many drawings of his wife and his sister, as well as models, which can only be compared with Gaudier, Matisse or Picasso. (Already some studies of his wife Frances, pregnant, in 1932, with their first daughter, Rachel, may be subliminally behind some aspects of the transformed and fantastic female imagery in certain wooden reliefs and one or two paintings of 1936–1938.)

But the drawings which, for most people, show Ceri's extraordinary powers of draughtsmanship are those later pencil studies of his father and his daughters made mostly in the nineteen forties and fifties (see catalogue nos II, III, VII, VIII, IX). These are among the most beautiful and tender drawings that I know of, made in my lifetime, and show such an extraordinary affection for the subjects that the integration between pencil mark and each component part of the form – hair, hand, eyes, the open watchfulness of expression or the absolute relaxation in sleep – seem to enter a new area of benign complicity between artist and sitter. The drawing of 'Rachel Writing', 1957 (catalogue no. IX) is worthy of Pissarro or Degas and although comparisons of this kind can be mislead-ing, it is true to say that very few drawings in this century contain this kind of absolute humanist belief in individual physical identity: even Picasso's great figurative drawings lean toward archetypal simplifi-cations – the agedness of an old woman, the unformed freshness and dreamy innocence of a girl or boy, and the drawings of Balthus although extraordinarily fine, are constricted by psychological pressures, eloquently so, but in a withdrawn, neurasthenic way that opposes the mood in Ceri's drawings. 'Rhiannon Asleep' 1946 (catalogue no. III) can, I believe, be considered with any of the great nineteenth century drawings, and it is odd that the instinct to place these drawings back in time is so strong. They seem to have a direct virtue which the post-Freud twentieth century has lost.

When Ceri left the Royal College, he had composed as a diploma piece in 1927 a painting of Piccadilly Circus at night, according to Alan Bowness (in his essay in the 1975 Edinburgh Festival C.R. exhibition catalogue), which was 'a very complex composition indebted to Duchamp and to futurism'. This is interesting as a fore-runner, at least in terms of the theme of a public metropolitan site, of his later and famous Trafalgar Square series of paintings, although the general approach is quite different. But what is most interesting is the apparent sophistication of Ceri's knowledge of the main preoccupations in contemporary art from a very early age. His move from the innocence and ignorance of modern issues in art, as a Welsh student, evidently was very fast. In later years, he was an inveterate collector of art books, beginning with *Cahiers d'Art* and *Minotaure*. He owned an important library of books on Picasso, and was well read in art theory, which he never followed because of the determining pressure of his own purely intuitive approach to art.

At the Royal College, Randolph Schwabe had been instrumental in opening his eyes to the possibilities of cubism, and at this time Ceri also read, with direct consequences, Kandinsky's 'On the Spiritual in Art'. Cubism provided him with the licence to explore a shape from different angles in the same picture, to break down an object and then reassemble the parts in a design of his own within a shallower space than the strictly perspectival spaces and distances of traditional representation. Kandinsky's theories opened Ceri's thinking to the possibility, delightful to Ceri, of making paintings which would have the same freedom as

music in the way in which forms and colour could be exploited for their own sakes. At this time, Ceri began to be familiar with the work of Matisse and Picasso.

His early works, between c.1930 and c.1934, often portraits of his wife or his sister, are very compact, decisive and economical paintings in which richly dark colours and, already, a sensuously varied painted surface combine to give a sense, almost, of modern French painting. The colour is personal from the beginning, ochres, deep reds, blue or yellow-greys, cinnamon, cornelian, blacks and creamy whites – often the deep colours of semi-precious stones, culminating in 'Blossoms' of 1940. But it is the relief constructions, made between 1934 and 1938, which form the first essential expansion and flowering of Ceri's mature talent. Some paintings of nudes, just earlier, which turn the female body into heavily contoured curving landscapes, still sexual, but also with the remoteness of a musical instrument, had begun the process of transformation from a compressed, Fauve-like simplification of form which was still faintly naturalistic to a more aggressive and expressive remodelling of form. But the reliefs pushed right out into the realm of surrealist fantasy, extending the freedom that Ceri was finding for himself in cubism and the theories of Kandinsky.

Ceri was on friendly terms with Ben Nicholson in the early thirties but apart from Ceri's general interest in abstract art, the real interests and pursuits of these artists had nothing in common. When Nicholson made his own reliefs, beginning in 1933, he wanted, among other things, to heighten and underline the physical reality of completely abstract form, pared down, as in Mondrian's paintings, to squares and rectangles which Nicholson built up into planes, with his own addition of circles. It is fairly clear that Ben Nicholson and Ceri both wanted to push beyond the boundaries of the flat picture plane itself, and to revivify what may have seemed even then to be the fatigue or the discredited illusionism of the conventional easel painting. But Nicholson pushed his reliefs outward, to more concretely architectonic elements which used light as an adjunct in a way that was new for modern art, although not of course unknown in Egyptian and Assyrian art.

Ceri's reliefs burrowed inward, and made his forms even more pictorial by turning his compositions into a kind of theatre, or theatrical tableaux, in which his shapes played out their own drama in a particularly contained, concentrated, formal and 'presented' way, as if they were inside a proscenium – the very opposite of Nicholson's preoccupations. Shadows were still painted, illusionistically, in Ceri's reliefs, although the whole impetus to make them had paradoxically flowed out of an intense period of preoccupation with the idea of making sculpture, earlier, in 1931. Ben Nicholson had not shown any interest in sculpture, and Arp's coloured reliefs of 1914 on should in any case be borne in mind as a possible technical example at that time for both Ceri and Ben Nicholson.

Julian Trevelyan, who was fond of Ceri and used to play the oboe in oboe and piano duets with him, recalls bringing Arp to see Ceri's reliefs in 1937. At this time, both Ceri and Trevelyan were seeing each other during that brief phase of English surrealism when it was already dying in Paris. Trevelyan had met Arp in 1931–1933, when he was living in Paris and working for S.W. Hayter the painter-engraver, in his recently established Atelier 17. In 1937, Arp expressed admiration for Ceri's reliefs but Trevelyan says also that contact between Arp and Ceri was difficult since neither man could speak the language of the other. (On this visit to London, one of Arp's strongest wishes was to visit the Tate to see illustrations by Arthur Rackham, on the advice of Breton, who saw Rackham as yet another precursor of surrealism.)

Ceri was certainly working with sculptural ideas in mind as early as 1931, when he made many drawings of sculptural themes and his interest in sculpture was encouraged by his friendship with Moore, and with McWilliam who, in a written note to me about Ceri, has said: 'We lost a great sculptor in Ceri, a view shared by Moore, for whom Ceri had great admiration. His sculptural interest was sublimated by his "sculptor at work" drawings of 1931, and of course by his reliefs, which were never properly appreciated here. Had he had a painting block, he might have turned to sculpture but I don't think he ever had.' Ceri's friendship with Moore is celebrated in 'The Sculptor's Landscape' 1943 which contains a portrait of Moore against 'inhabited' rocks, and derives in colour and structure from memories of the Gower peninsular.

The wooden reliefs extend the principles of cubism and the cubist collages made by Picasso in 1917 into something much grander and more ceremonial. Each relief has the explicit tension of a 'scene', an exact economy and equation between ends and means and tight variations between constricted, compacted forms and very expansive detail, like plays with perfect plots. The reliefs are also very finely crafted and have an oddly affectionate mood of good husbandry and a warm attention to eccentricities of detail.

Of special significance is the way in which the character of the form in the reliefs changes from the drily compressed and simplified cubist shapes in 'Piano' 1934 (catalogue no. 1) to the more sensuously curving, rounded, flowing and surrealistically disruptive, ornamental nature of the two constructed personages in 'Two Females' 1937–8 (catalogue no. 8). These personages reflect an awareness of Ernst's surrealist imagery, as much as Picasso's, but they are also quite personal to Ceri and establish, with the shapes in the painting 'The Female Contains All Qualities' of 1937 (catalogue no. 15) some of his most characteristic imagery. In this relief and in the painting, the characteristic form of a disc, flower, boss, circle or mandala is established which floats through much subsequent work, from 'Blossoms' 1940 (catalogue no. 34 inspired by the artist's reaction to Ciano's cynical comment about the 'beauty' of bombs bursting over Abyssinia), right through to the 'Cathédrale Engloutie' paintings, collages and drawings of 1959 onwards. Jung owned for many years a painted study for the

1952 'Black Apple of Gower' painting, celebrating abstractly a Welsh legend in a large mandala.

Given these clues, the rest of Ceri's work really explains itself. He likes to explore themes, for in the way that his drawing always opened up a subject rather than sealed it off, each painting left possibilities for later development through their prolixity and emphasis on movement and flux rather than static containment. It is not difficult to follow the ebb and flow of development from the paintings inspired by the poem by Dylan Thomas – he and Ceri met only once, just before Dylan's last visit to America – which begins 'The force that through the green fuse drives the flower' to the 'Cycle of Nature' paintings. Here, Ceri's flair for creating metaphor is most strikingly at work, fusing together vegetable and human references with images which refer to procreation and the forces of growth and death.

The long series of paintings of pianists in interiors made in the late forties and fifties register most clearly Ceri's love of music and the way in which figurative or illusionistic elements, often in these paintings the musician or the listener, rather than their context, are set against abstract inventions, reintegrated by the authority of the design and typical, in McWilliam's phrase, of 'the idea of a symbiosis or reconciliation latent in a lot of his work'. These paintings and drawings, usually based on observation of his daughters, are among the most characteristic and strongly felt works.

The Trafalgar Square paintings are among Ceri's most popular works, in all the meanings of the word, and are indeed full of a sense of celebration, stimulated as they were by an exhibition organised by the Arts Council to coincide with the Festival of Britain, which specified large paintings. But the paintings which contain some of Ceri's finest inventions are in the 'Cathédrale Engloutie' series. The 1910 piano prelude of Debussy inspired Ceri for several years and persuaded him also to explore again the possibilities of constructed reliefs which, in the sixties, became far

more decorative, serenely or ebulliently so, than the earlier works. The legend of Ys and its submerged cathedral with the sound of its bell and organ sounding from the depths, yielded a marvellously varied series of variations on the visual equivalent of sonority, rise and fall and eddying of currents, the sharply contoured flash of light across water, together with fragments of gothic arches, rose windows and decorated capitals. The greens and blues and sand colours of these paintings make their own world, just as decisively as the bright reds and greens of the earlier cycle of nature paintings; and the rounded whorls of sand and flowing water and the rounded sections of pillars that he imagined, on the ocean bed, like millstones, signal back twenty years to the round bursting aerial blossoms of 1940.

One of the most affecting elements in all Ceri's paintings is the sense of shadow in midsummer, a sense perhaps of mortality which finds itself in the subdued tonalities that fortify Ceri's most effulgent celebration of life and nature. Later paintings were free of this shadow: perhaps its last appearance is in the black swan which Ceri invented for his 'Music of Colours' paintings that were suggested by the Vernon Watkins poem 'Music of Colours – White Blossom'. (Watkins was a friend and neighbour on the Gower peninsular where Ceri had a summer cottage in later years.)

The paintings which followed, in the late sixties, became brighter and clearer in colour and very toughly composed, full of an almost superabundant energy, with bristling images of seed pods, swelling mounds of earth and other symbols of regeneration, but are more flat in their composition than earlier paintings, in which forms are always set in a shallow space as well as in atmospheric density. For Ceri, tonality had a temporal presence, equivocating and modifying as well as creating another dimension, and sometimes disrupting through an illusion of solidity an otherwise abstract concept. Ceri liked to have a foot in both worlds.

The Force that Through the Green Fuse

The force that through the green fuse drives the flower
Drives my green age; that blasts the roots of trees
Is my destroyer.
And I am dumb to tell the crooked rose
My youth is bent by the same wintry fever.

The force that drives the water through the rocks
Drives my red blood; that dries the mouthing streams
Turns mine to wax.
And I am dumb to mouth unto my veins
How at the mountain spring the same mouth sucks.

The hand that whirls the water in the pool
Stirs the quicksand; that ropes the blowing wind
Hauls my shroud sail.
And I am dumb to tell the hanging man
How of my clay is made the hangman's lime.

The lips of time leech to the fountain head;
Love drips and gathers, but the fallen blood
Shall calm her sores.
And I am dumb to tell a weather's wind
How time has ticked a heaven round the stars.

And I am dumb to tell the lover's tomb
How at my sheet goes the same crooked worm.

Dylan Thomas

White blossom, white, white shell; the Nazarene
Walking in the ear; white touched by souls
Who know the music by which white is seen,
Blinding white, from strings and aureoles,
Until that is not white, seen at the two poles,
Nor white the Scythian hills, nor Marlowe's queen.

The spray looked white until this snowfall.
Now the foam is grey, the wave is dull.
Call nothing white again, we were deceived.
The flood of Noah dies, the rainbow is lived.
Yet from the deluge of illusions an unknown colour is saved.

White must die black, to be born white again
From the womb of sounds, the inscrutable grain,
From the crushed, dark fibre, breaking in pain.

The bud of the apple is already forming there.
The cherry-bud, too, is firm, and behind it the pear
Conspires with the racing cloud. I shall not look.
The rainbow is diving through the wide-open book
Past the rustling paper of birch, the sorceries of bark.

Buds in April on the waiting branch,
Starrily opening, light raindrops drench,
Swinging from world to world when starlings sweep,
Where they alight in air, are white asleep.
They will not break, not break, until you say
White is not white again, nor may may.

White flowers die soonest, die into that chaste
Bride-bed of the moon, their lives laid waste.
Lilies of Solomon, taken by the gust,
Sigh, make way. And the dark forest
Haunts the lowly crib near Solomon's dust,
Rocked to the end of majesty, warmed by the low beast,
Locked in the liberty of his tremendous rest.

If there is white, or has been white, it must have been
When His eyes looked down and made the leper clean.
White will not be, apart, though the trees try
Spirals of blossom, their green conspiracy.
She who touched His garment saw no white tree.

Lovers speak of Venus, and the white doves,
Jubilant, the white girl, myth's whiteness, Jove's,
Of Leda, the swan, whitest of his loves.
Lust imagines him, web-footed Jupiter, great down
Of thundering light; love's yearning pulls him down
On the white swan-breast, the magical lawn,
Involved in plumage, mastered by the veins of dawn.

In the churchyard the yew is neither green nor black.
I know nothing of Earth or colour until I know I lack
Original white, by which the ravishing bird looks wan.
The mound of dust is nearer, white of mute dust that dies
In the soundfall's great light, the music in the eyes,
Transfiguring whiteness into shadows gone,
Utterly secret. I know you, black swan.

Vernon Watkins

A Biographical Chronology

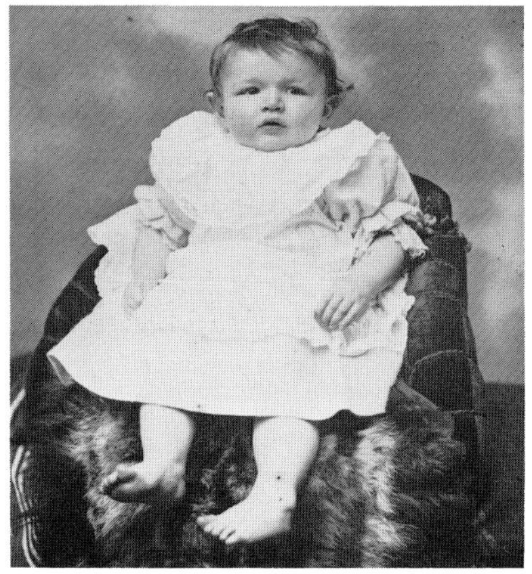

The artist, aged eighteen months

1903

Ceri Giraldus Richards was born in Dunvant, a small mining village near Swansea, on the edge of the Gower peninsula, of Welsh-speaking parents and antecedents. The landscape of Gower with its limestone cliffs and headlands, sandy estuaries, and the sea around it, provided Richards with a source of imagery at several periods in his career ('Rocks' 1942; 'The Sculptor's Landscape' 1943; the 'Cathédrale Engloutie' paintings; 'Music of Colours, White Blossom' 1968 etc.)

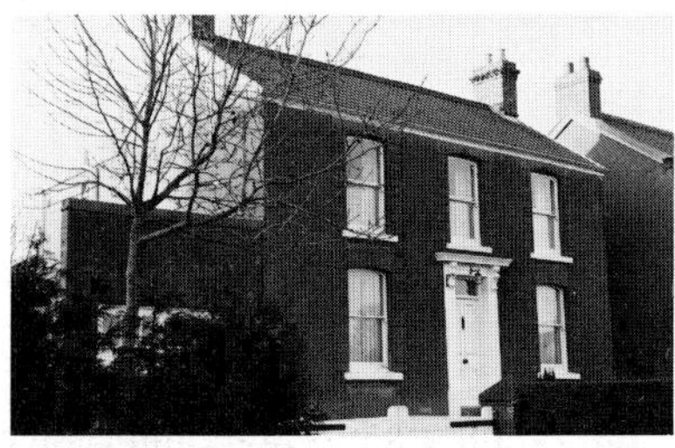

Preswylfa, Dunvant, birthplace and childhood home

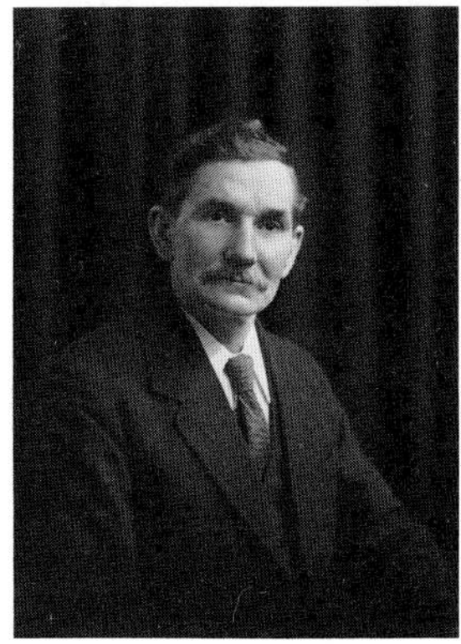

The artist's father Thomas Richards

His father, a tin-plate worker, had a deep love of music and poetry, and encouraged his family in these arts. Ceri learned early to play the piano, and as a boy played the organ for the local chapel. Music was to be an abiding preoccupation and a continuous inspiration to his art.

1919

After leaving Gowerton Grammar School he became apprenticed to a local electrical engineering firm, attending classes in technical drawing and art.

1921

Enrolled as a full-time student at Swansea School of Art, where he received generous encouragement from his teachers.

1923

First saw the collection of the Davies sisters at Gregynog; the Daumiers and especially the late Monets came as a revelation to him.

1924

Scholarship to the Royal College of Art. First contact with Modernism through Professor Randolph Schwabe who introduced him to Apollinaire's *Les Peintres Cubistes*, and Kandinsky's *Concerning the Spiritual in Art*, which affected him deeply. First experience of Picasso and Matisse. At the College his remarkable gift for drawing was widely recognised by teachers and fellow students.

1927

Illustrated *The Magic Horse* (from The Arabian Nights) for Gollancz. Began work as a commercial artist for the London Press Association.

Frances Richards 1938

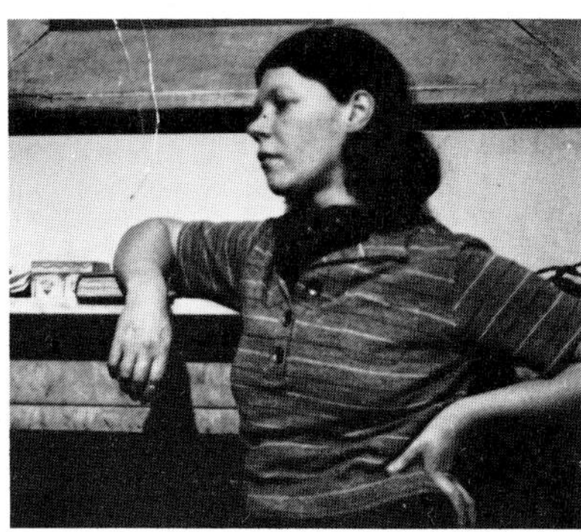

1929

Married to Frances Clayton, who had been a contemporary at the R C A. Lived in Fulham Road, London.

1930

First one-man show at Glynn Vivian Art Gallery, Swansea. At this period he became friends with David Jones, and with the poet John Tessimond, with whom he worked at the London Press Association. Tessimond introduced him to Debussy, Ravel and other modern French composers.

1932

Birth of his daughter, Rachel.

1933

Became interested in relief construction and collage and began to experiment in these media. Exhibited with the Objective Abstractionist Group (which included Pasmore, Hitchens and Moynihan) at the Zwemmer Gallery, London.

1935–6

Interested throughout this period in the possibilities of sculpture and sculptural 'objects'. In 1936 exhibited free-standing 'object' with Surrealist Group at London Gallery; c.1936 bought Ernst's 'Bride of the Wind'.

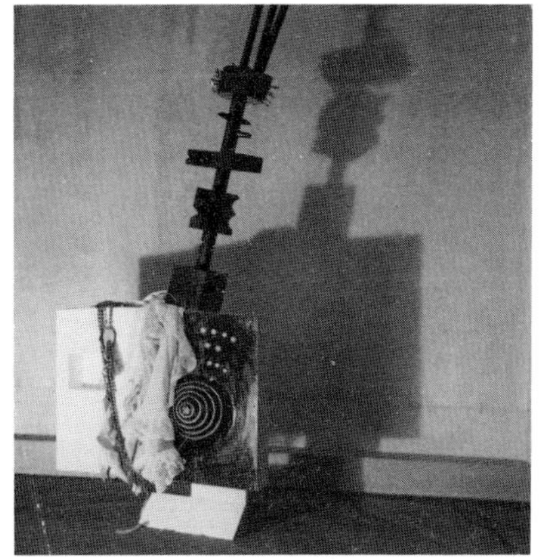

Surrealist 'object' exhibited 1936

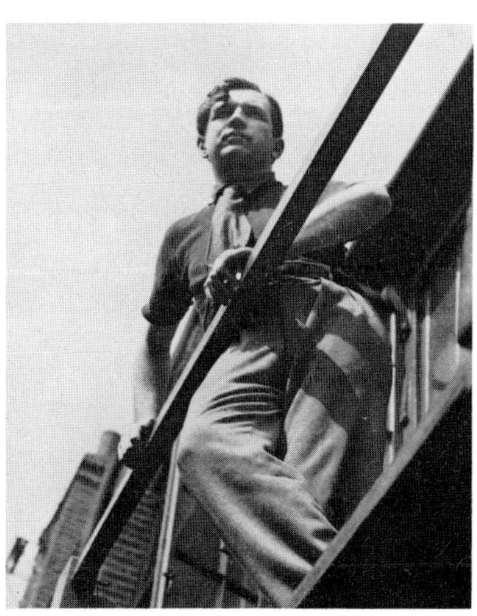

Ceri Richards 1936

1937

Elected member of London Group; exhibited relief constructions for the first time. Arp visited the artist's studio in St Peter's Square, Hammersmith and expressed great admiration for the reliefs. At this time Richards gave up commercial work and took up a part-time post at Chelsea College of Art, where his colleagues included Henry Moore and Graham Sutherland. Commissioned by Colin Anderson to design relief construction for SS *Orcades*.

1939

At the outbreak of war, and following the consequent closure of London Art Schools, he moved briefly to Suffolk, and from there to Cardiff.

1940–1

Firewatcher with ARP in Cardiff during the period of bombing (see 'Blossoms' 1940; and 'Falling Forms' 1944).

Cardiff 1940

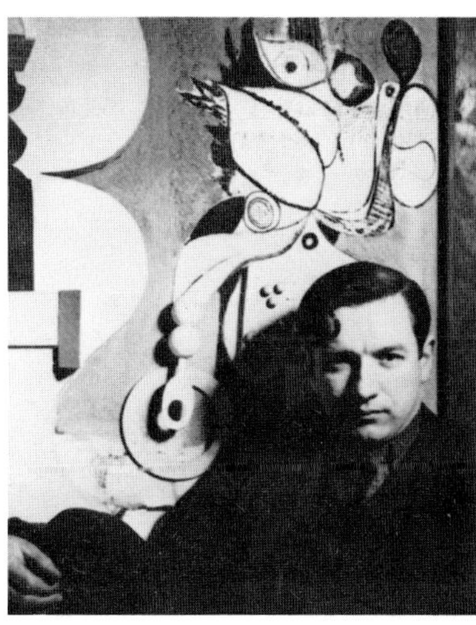

1940–44

Head of Painting at Cardiff School of Art.

1942

First one-man show in London at the Leger Gallery.

1943

Commissioned by Ministry of Information to make drawings of tin-plate workers in South Wales.

1943/4

During this period Richards's interest in the poetry of Dylan Thomas deepened, intensified by a commission to make a lithographic illustration of 'The force that through the green fuse' for Tambimuttu's *Poetry London*. (This was the first lithograph that Richards made).

Fascinated by the energy and compositional complexity of Delacroix's 'The Lion Hunt' Richards began a series of free painted paraphrases of that painting. He returned to this subject frequently (he exhibited a number of oils on this theme at the Marlborough Gallery in 1963).

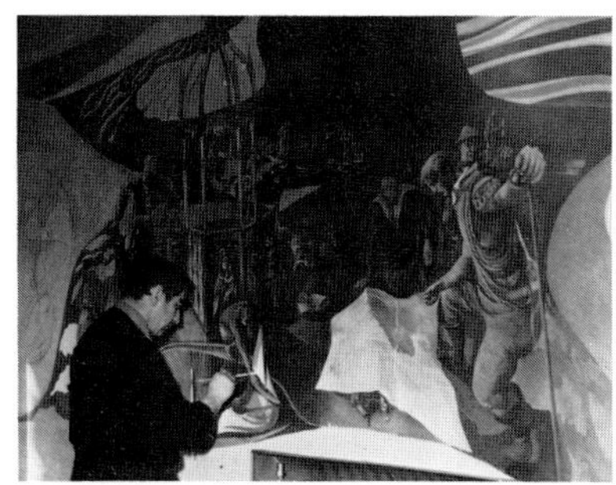

Painting Norwegian mural, Cardiff 1944

1944

Commissioned by the Royal Norwegian Government in exile to paint murals with appropriate motif in Norwegian Room at the premises of the British Council in Wales, in Caroline Street, Cardiff.

1945

Birth of his second daughter, Rhiannon. The war over, the family moved back to London, to a house on Wandsworth Common, where Richards began a long series of paintings on the themes of the 'Pianist' and the 'Interior of a room'. Resumed teaching at Chelsea.

1947

Found in the 'Sabine' theme a subject that gave full play to his obsession with figurative drawing. Monoprints on this theme made at this time as well as lithographs and paintings. Friendship with Robert Medley, Rupert Doone, Victor Pasmore, Francis Bacon.

1951

Contributed large 'Trafalgar Square' (now in Tate Gallery) to Festival exhibition *Sixty Paintings for '51*.

1952

Richards fell seriously ill and underwent surgery. The hospital experience prompted a series of paintings, and the theme, to which he often returned, of the inert figure wrapped in a winding sheet. ('Return of the Patient' 1953; 'Do not go gentle . . .' 1956; 'The Deposition' 1958).

1953

Death of Dylan Thomas. The poet and painter met on only one occasion, the day before Thomas's last journey to America, to discuss collaboration on a poetry reading. Richards, however, had strongly identified with the poetry of his fellow Welshman, and felt his death deeply. ('The Black Apple of Gower' 1952).

1954

Designed drop-cloth for the memorial reading of works by Dylan Thomas at the Globe Theatre, London. A number of elegiac studies for this survive. Exhibition *Homage to Two Poets* at Glynn Vivian Art Gallery, Swansea, for Dylan Thomas and Vernon Watkins. Designed mural for Orient Line SS *Orsova*. Entered prize-winning lithograph at 3rd Mostra Internazionale di Bianco e Nero at Lugano. Teaching lithography at Slade School, where Stanley Jones was among his students.

Working on school mural, Worthing 1955 (since painted over)

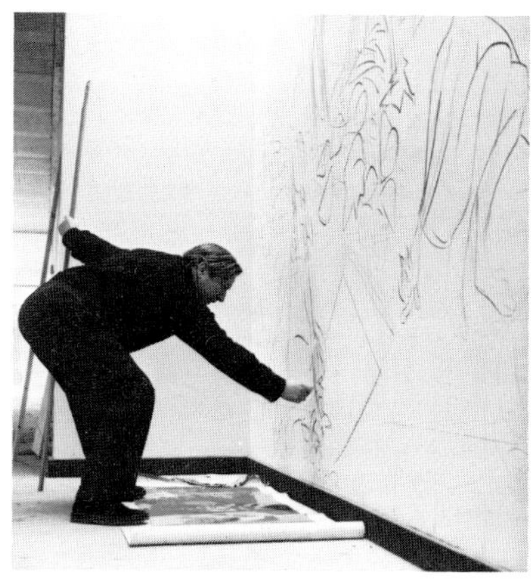

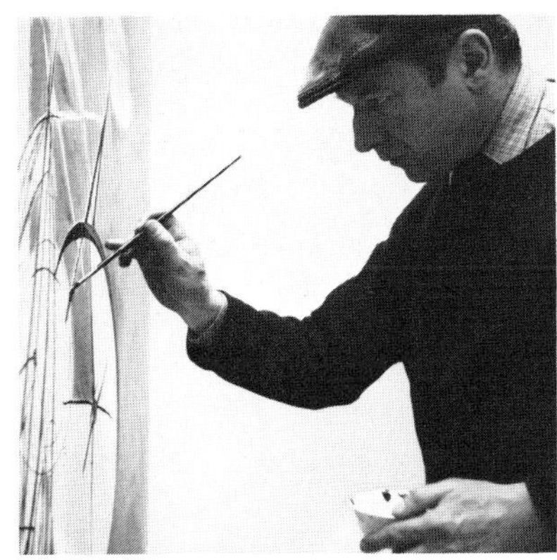

Sanesi at the Pennard home of Vernon Watkins. Made Trustee of the Tate Gallery.

1959

Prize at John Moores. 'Hammerklavier' lithograph wins a prize at 3rd International Exhibition of Prints, Ljubljana. Working throughout late fifties and early sixties on the 'Cathédrale Engloutie' theme, inspired by the Debussy prelude.

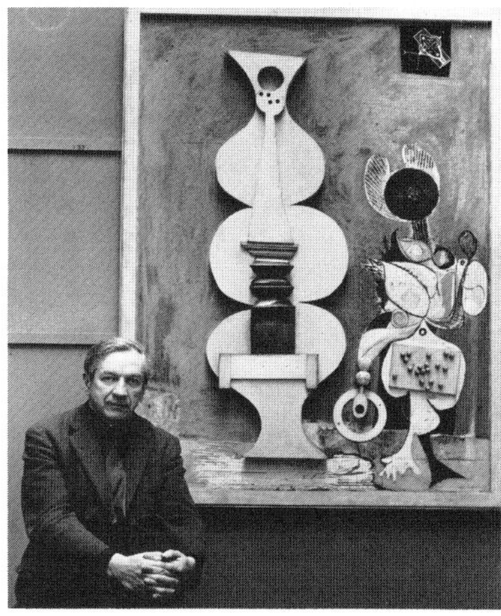

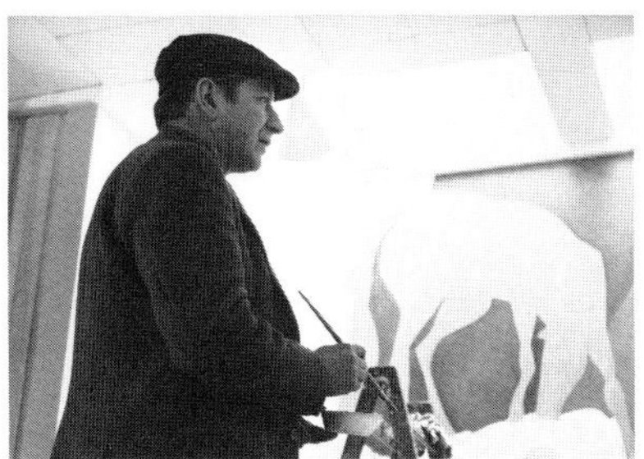

Working on school mural, Worthing 1955

1956

Designed decor and costumes for *Ruth* by Lennox Berkeley, produced by the English Opera Group at the Scala Theatre.

1957

Prize at John Moores Liverpool Exhibition.

1958

Designed the costumes and masks for *Noyes Fludde* by Benjamin Britten, which was performed at the Aldeburgh Festival. Commissioned to paint Altarpiece for St Edmund Hall, Oxford. Met the Italian poet and critic, Roberto

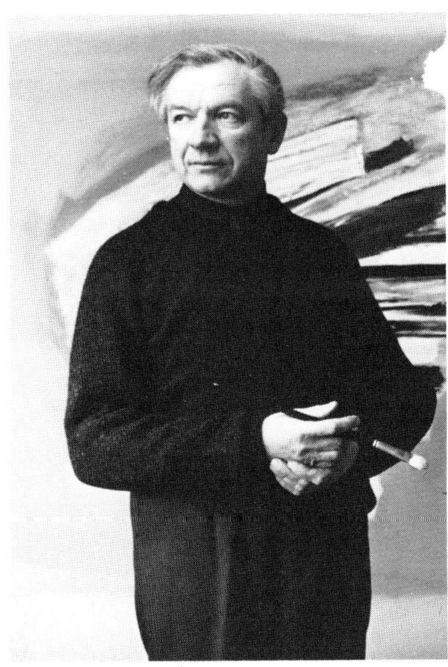

Ceri Richards 1959

1960

Major retrospective exhibition at Whitechapel Gallery. Awarded CBE.

1961

Honorary degree of D. Litt, University of Wales. Honorary Fellow of Royal College of Art, London. Gold Medal, Royal National Eisteddfod, Wales.

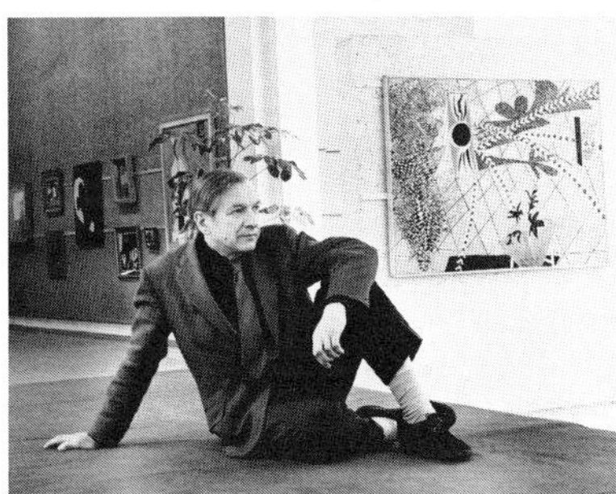

Whitechapel, Retrospective 1960

1962

Retrospective exhibition at Venice Biennale, where he was awarded Einaudi Prize for Painting.

1964

Designed two large stained glass windows for Derby Cathedral.

1965

Made *12 lithographs for 6 Poems by Dylan Thomas* at Curwen Studio with

[25]

Stanley Jones, a major suite recapitulating the Dylan Thomas themes. Executed large painting ('Armada') for Shakespeare Festival exhibition.

1967

Death of Richards's great friend Vernon Watkins. In the early sixties Richards had bought a cottage on the clifftops at Pennard in Gower where Watkins lived, and the painter and poet had spent much time together. Richards wrote later 'Now that he is not there any more the environment seems deprived and inarticulate.' (*Remembering Vernon* in *Vernon Watkins 1906–1967*. 'Music of Colours – White Blossom (Requiem for a Poet)' 1968).

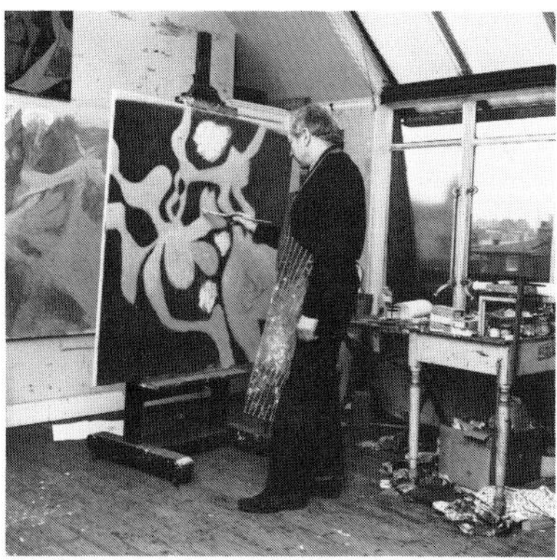

The artist in his Chelsea studio 1968

1968

Awarded Gold Medal (best foreign painter) at the International Exhibition of Contemporary Art, Delhi. Designed the windows and tabernacle, and painted reredos for the Chapel of the Blessed Sacrament in the Cathedral of Christ the King, Liverpool.

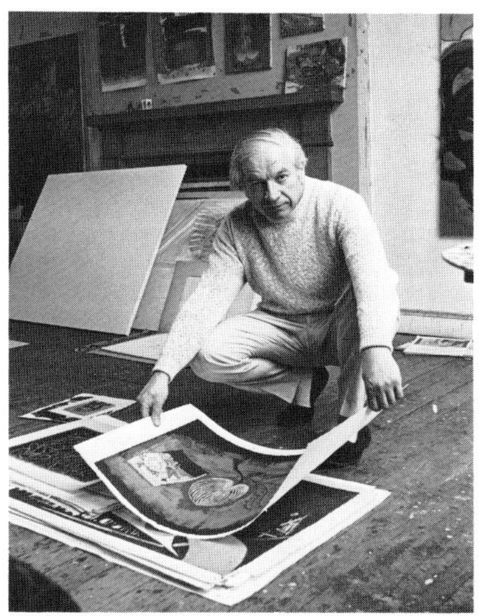

Ceri Richards, Chelsea 1971

1970

'Beethoven Suite with Variations' published; a portfolio of screenprints created at Kelpra Studios in celebration of the bi-centenary of the birth of Beethoven, Richards's favourite composer.

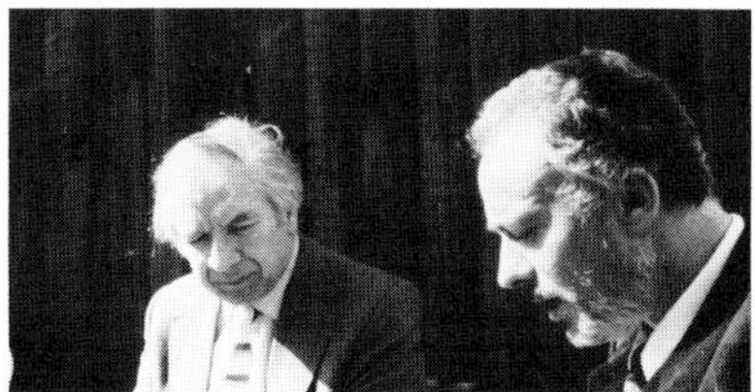

With Roberto Sanesi, Chelsea 1971

1971

Lithographic illustrations to Folio edition of *Under Milk Wood* by Dylan Thomas edited by Douglas Cleverdon, published posthumously (1972). Lithographs for Roberto Sanesi's book of poems *Journey toward the North* – the artist's last work, also published posthumously (1972), in Italy.

Ceri Richards died in London, 9 November 1971.

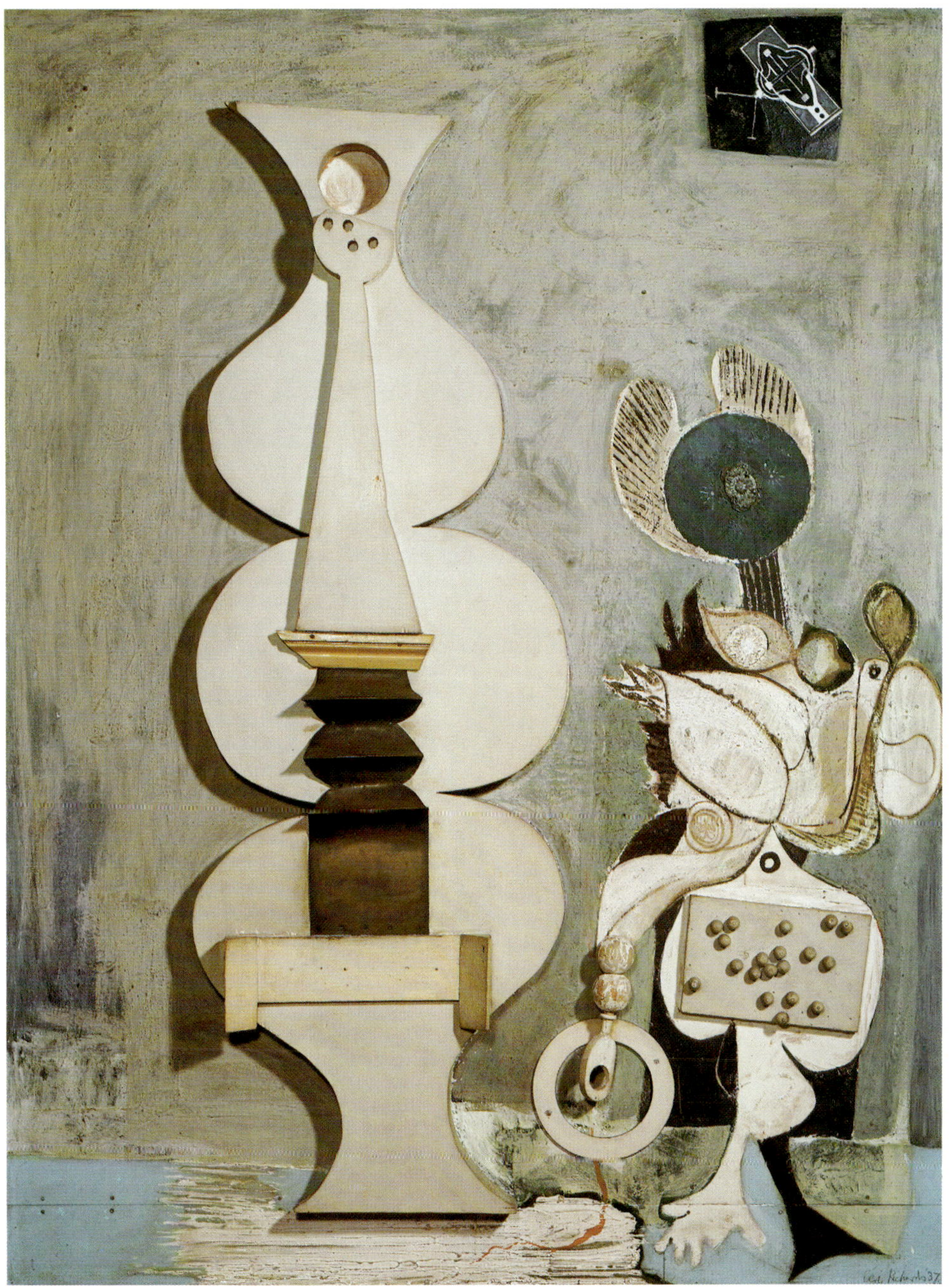

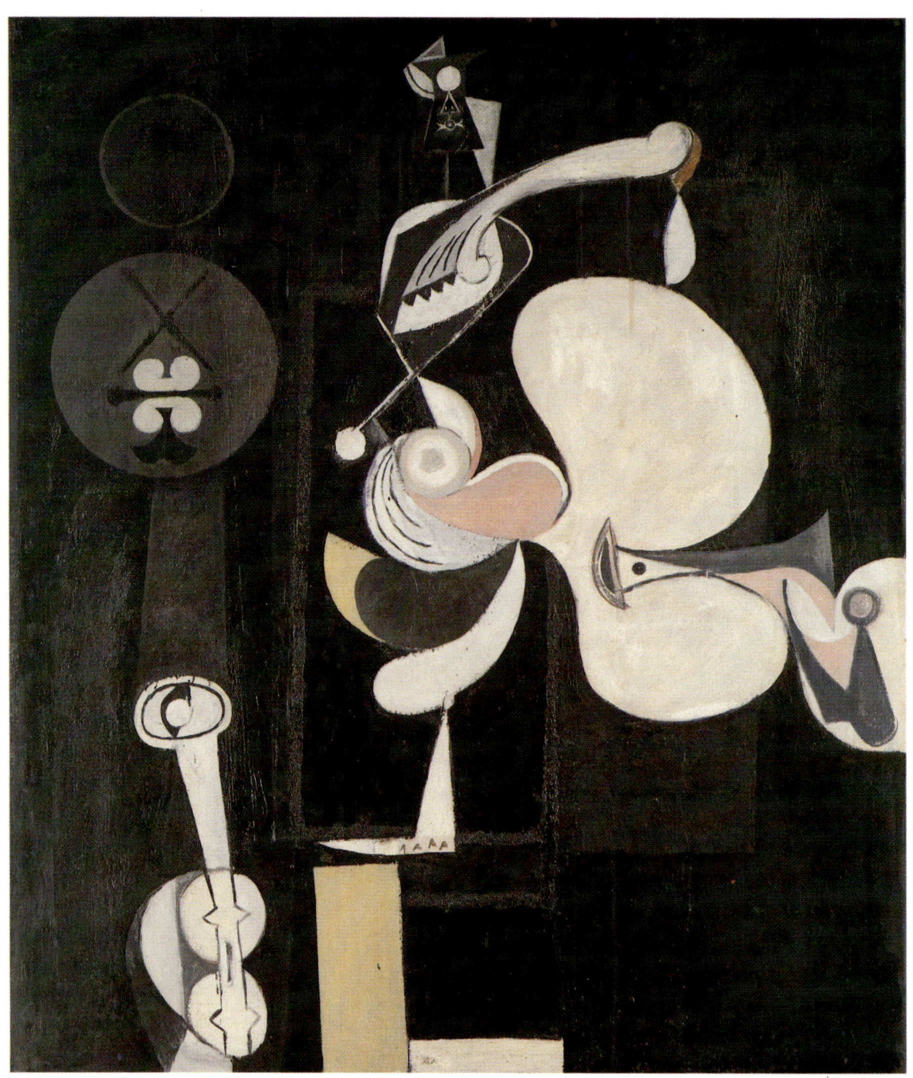

15 **The Female Contains
All Qualities** 1938

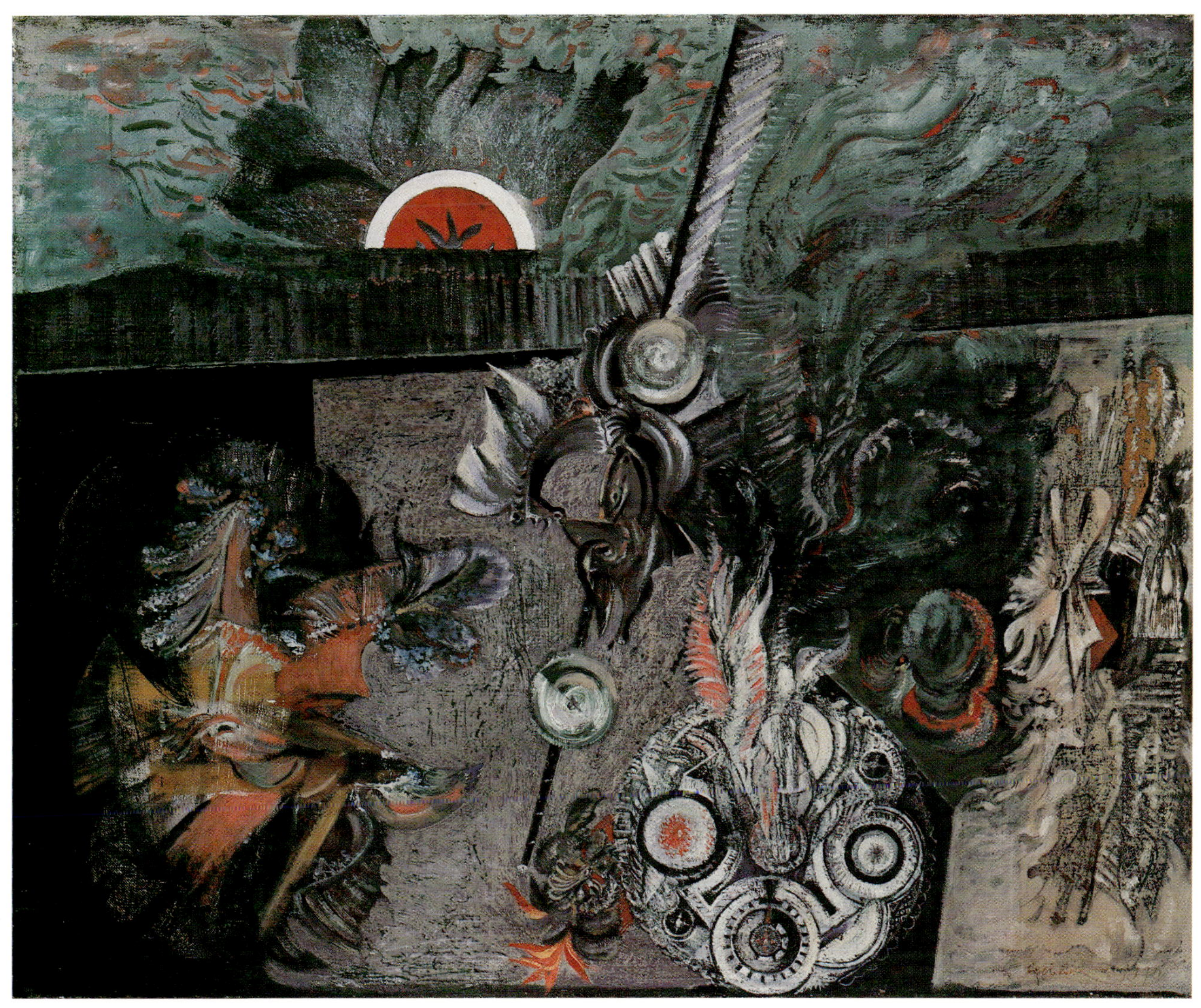

34 **Blossoms** 1940

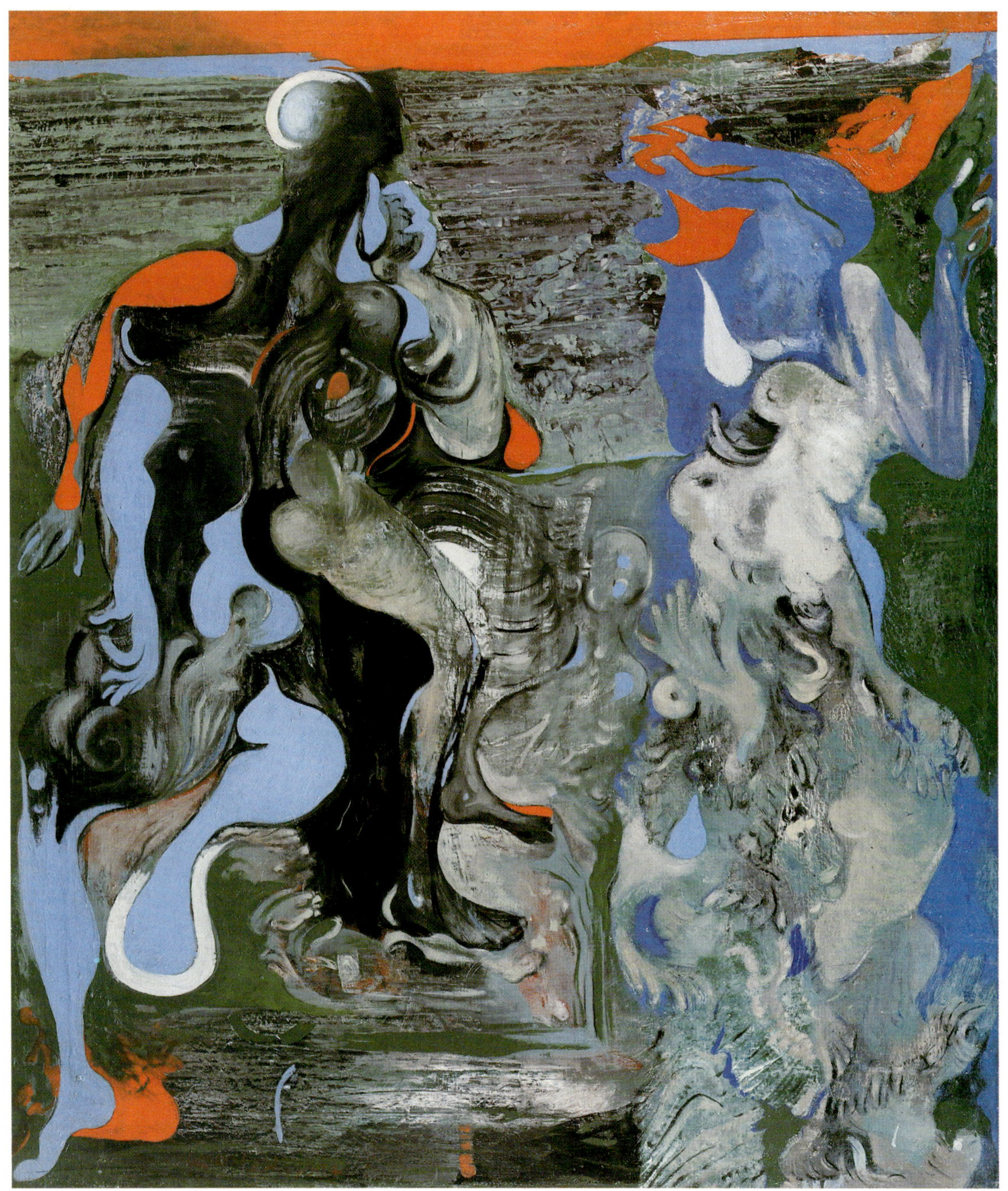

[30]

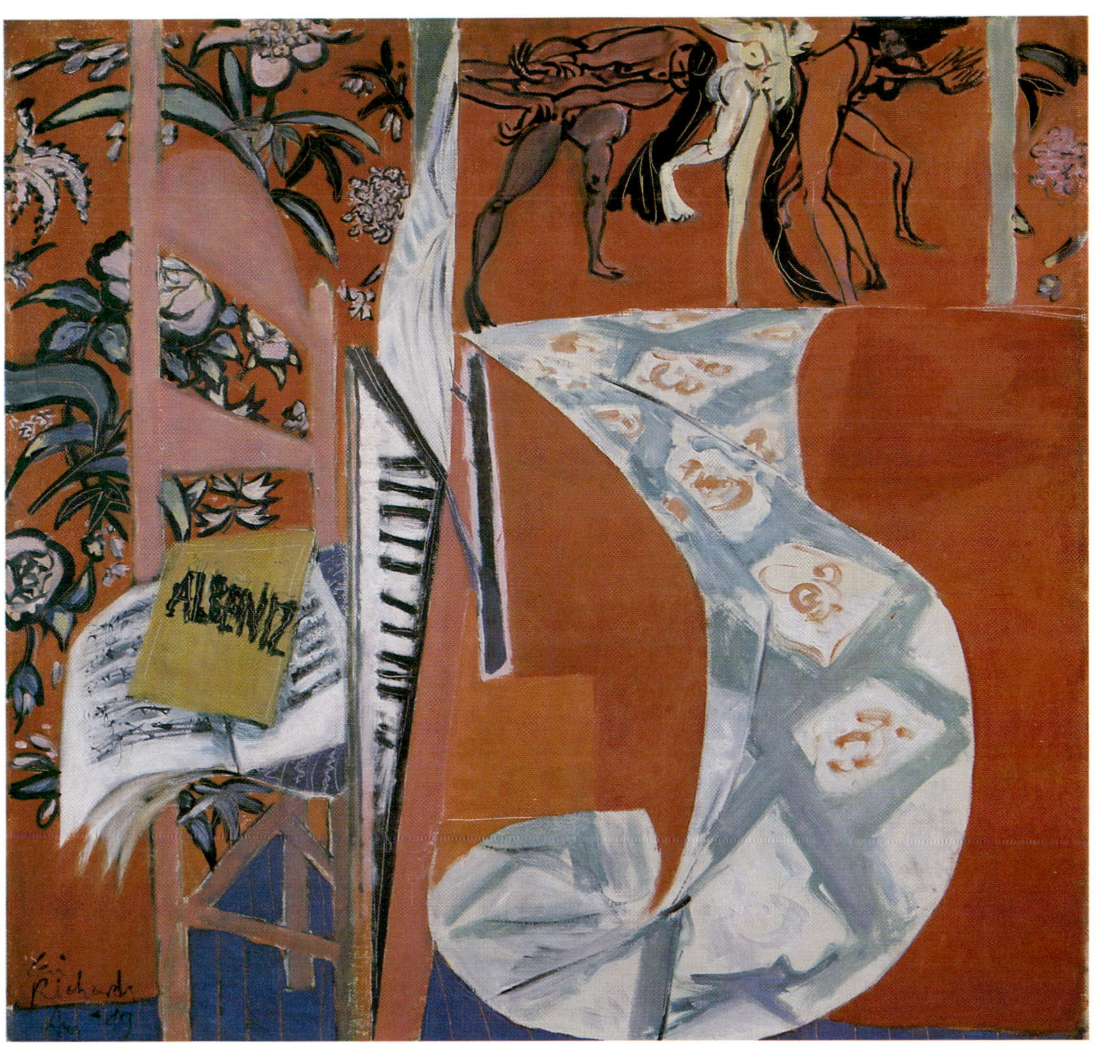

45 Red Interior with Music
by Albeniz 1949

opposite

40 'The force that drives the
water through the rock
drives my red
blood' 1943/4

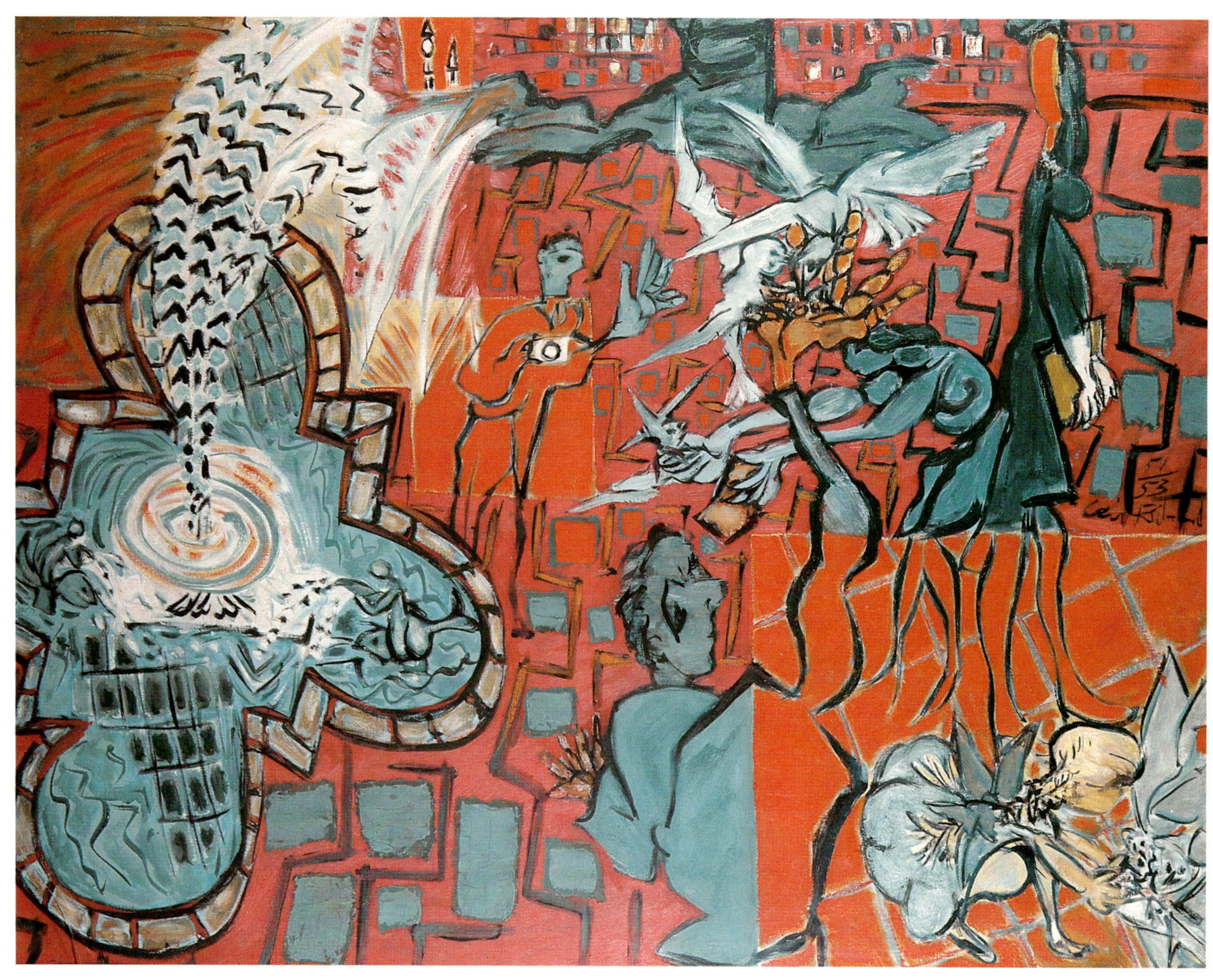

57 **Trafalgar Square** 1951–53

71 La Cathédrale Engloutie I
1959

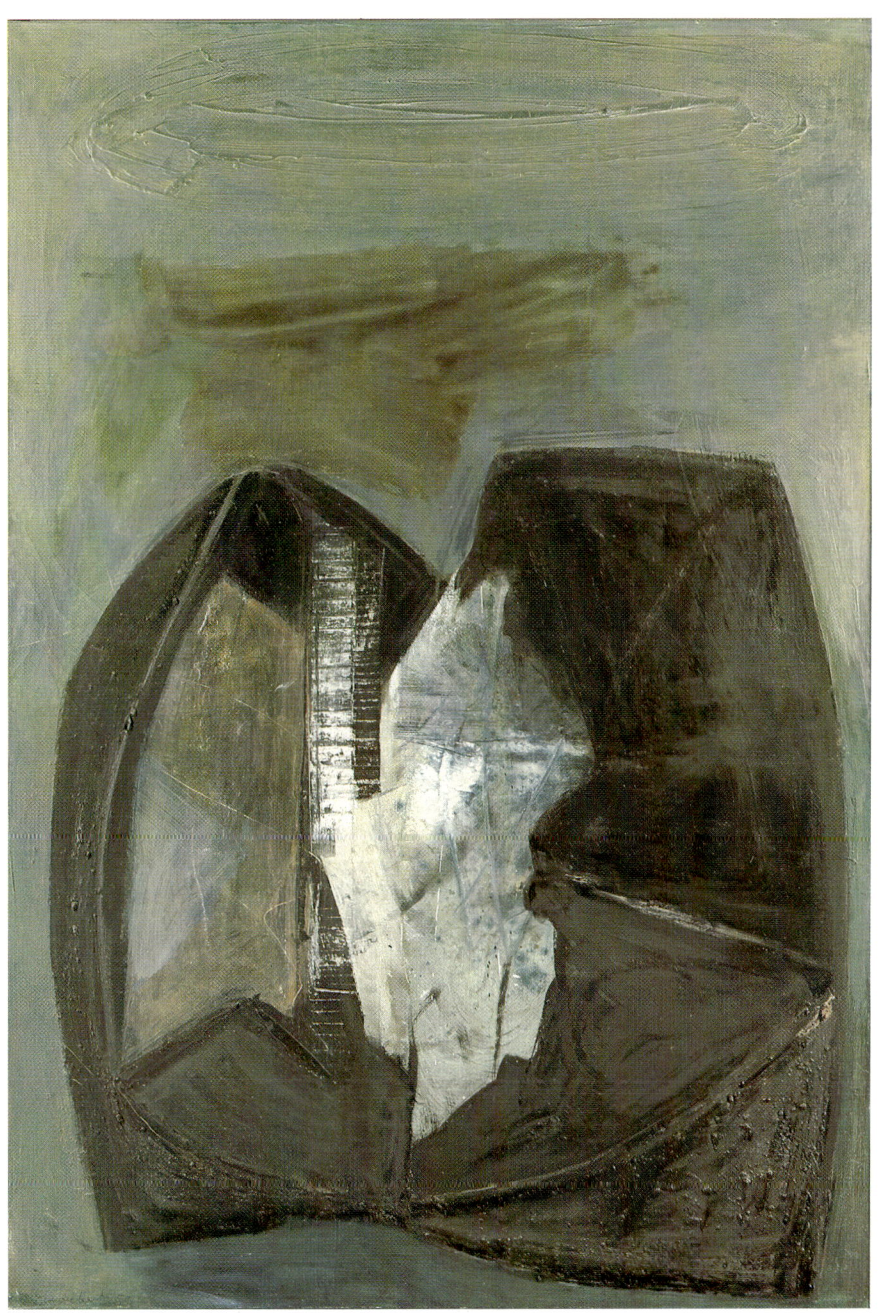

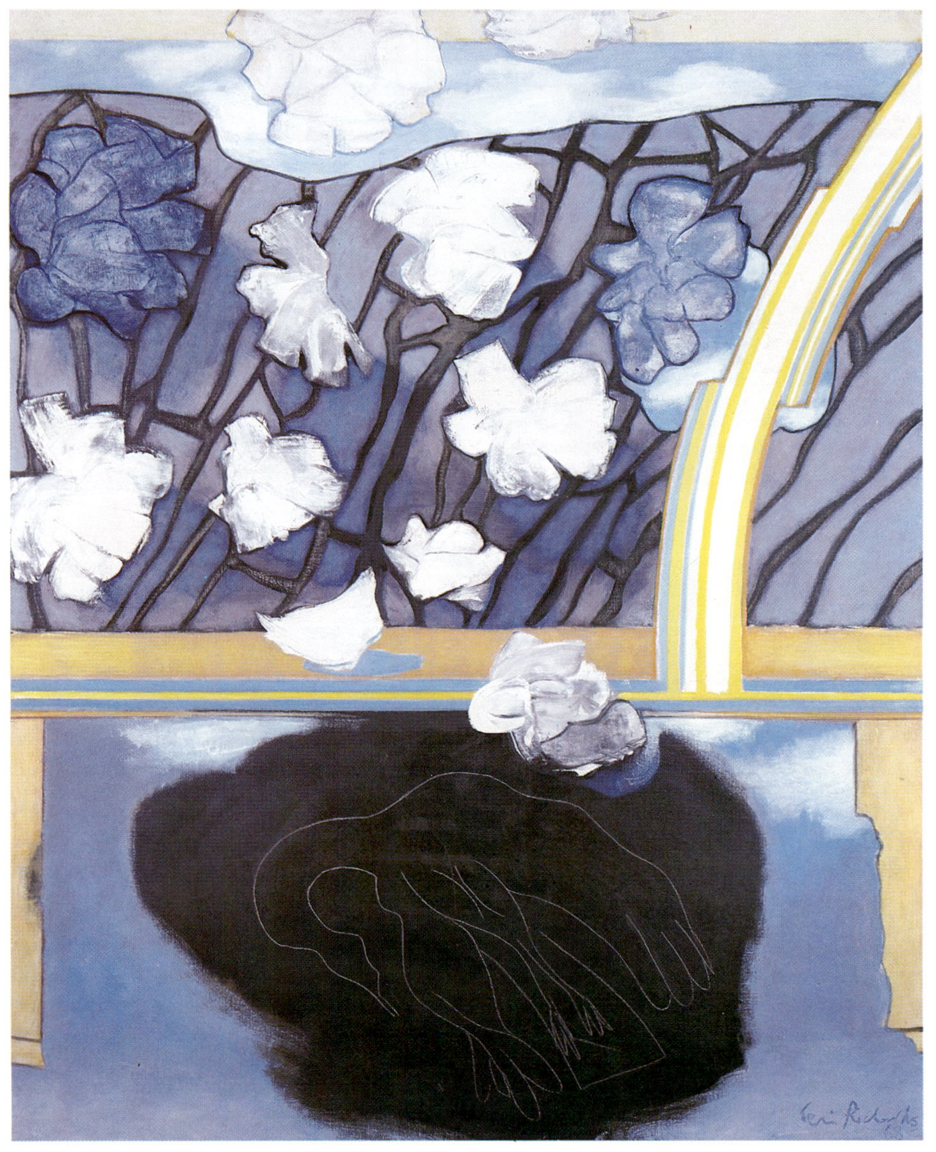

91 **Music of colours – White Blossom (Requiem for a Poet)** 1968

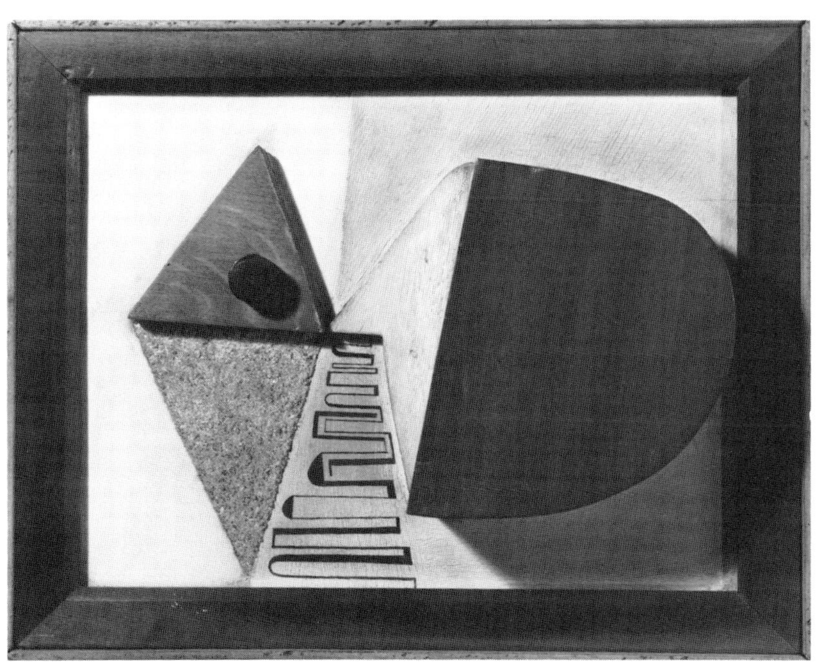

1 Piano 1934

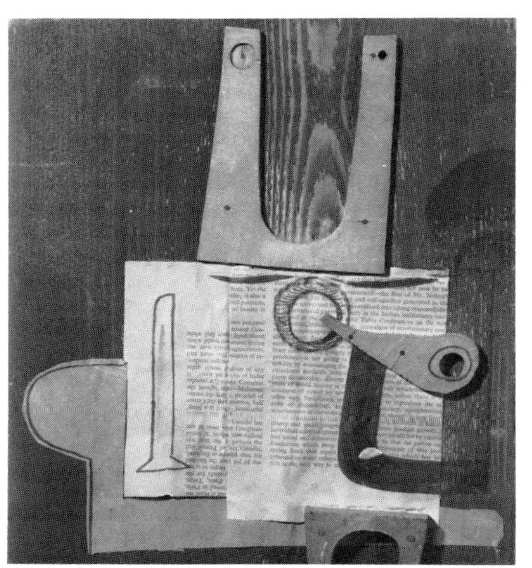

2 Man with a Pipe 1934

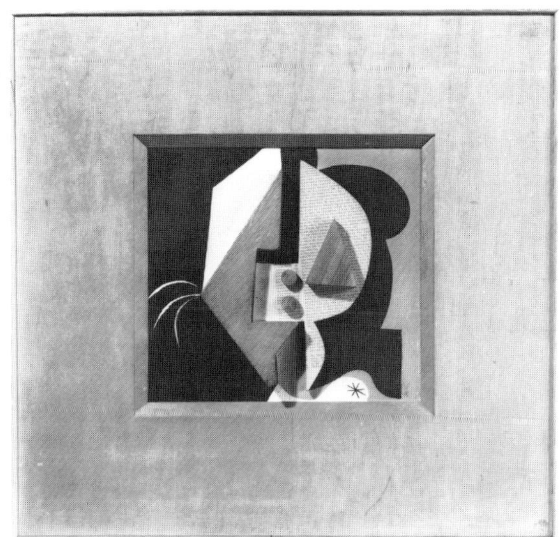

4 Head 1935

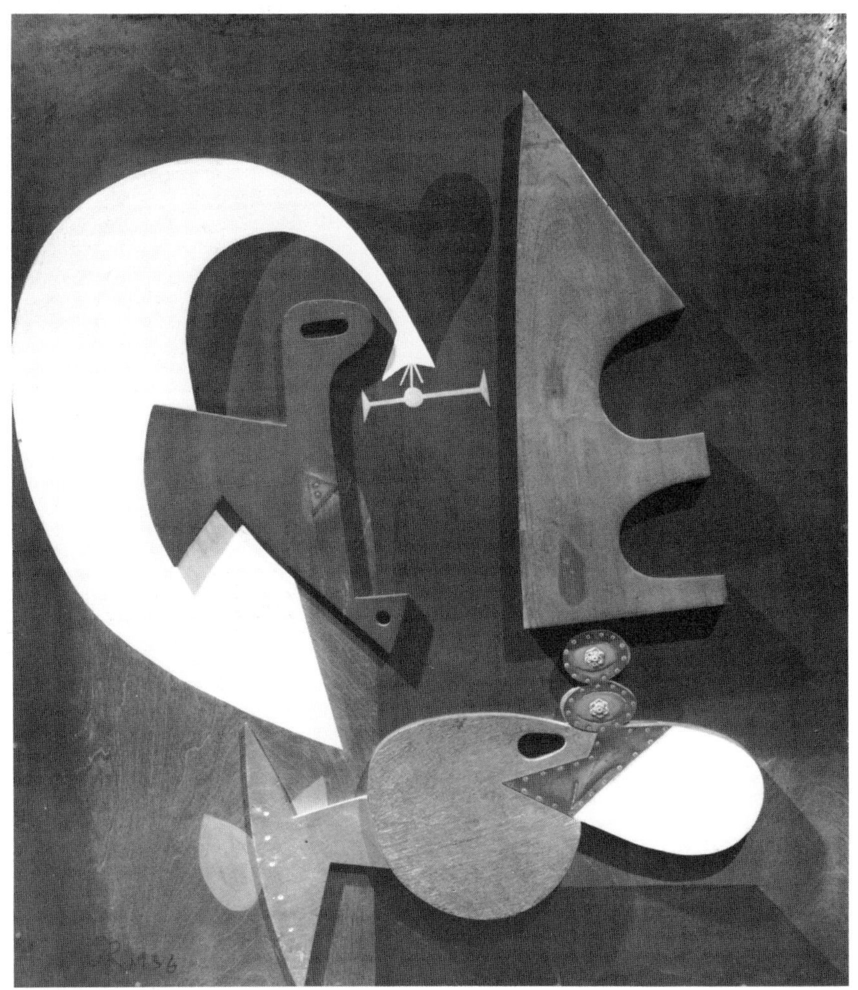

6 **The Sculptor and his
   Model** 1936

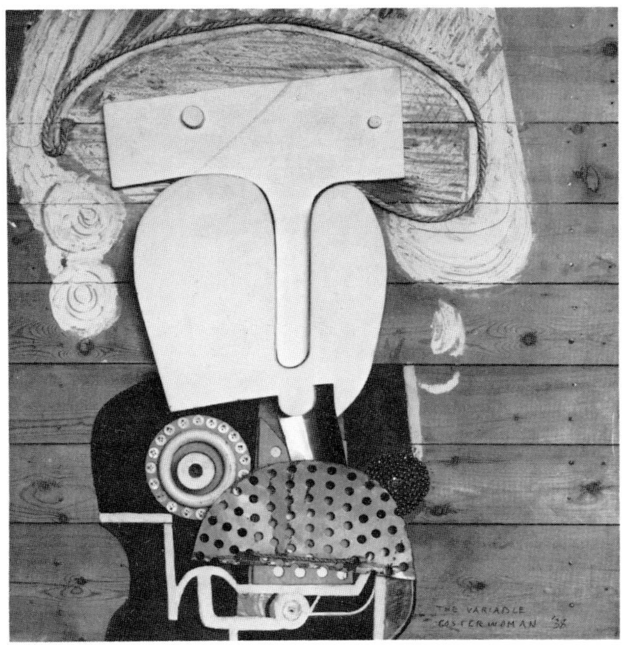

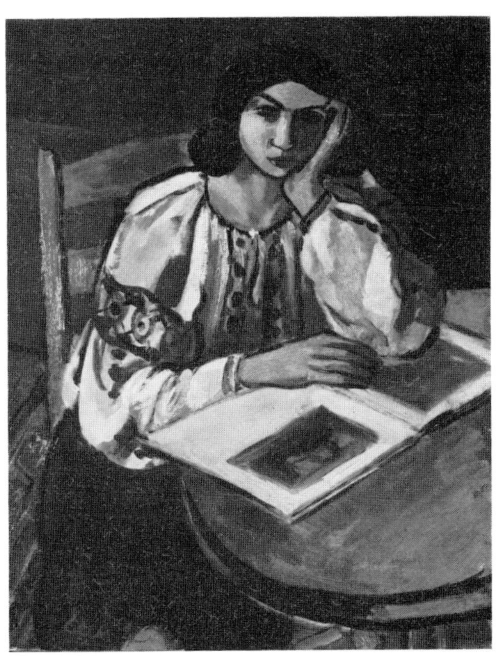

above
10 **The Variable
Costerwoman** 1938

above right
11 **Portrait of the Artist's
Sister** 1932

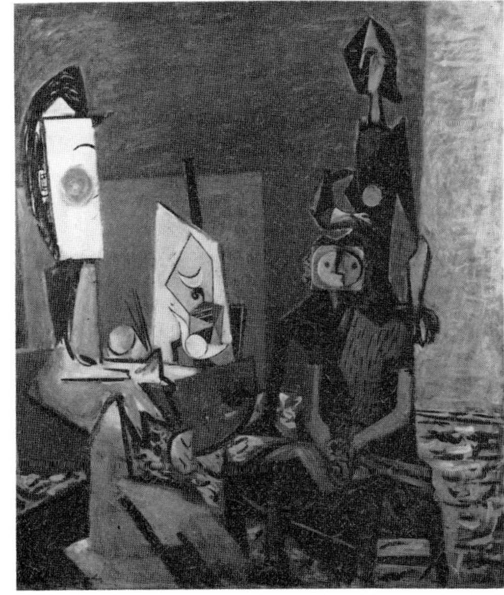

14 **The Artist and his
Model** 1937

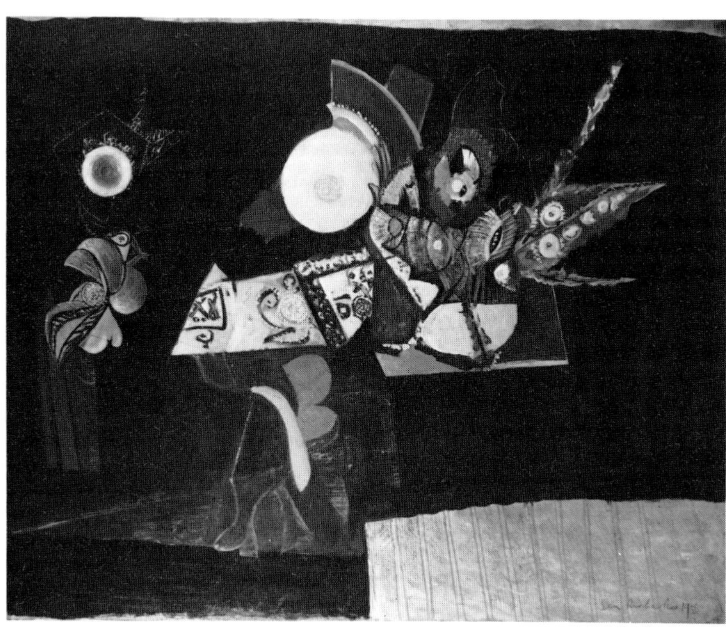

16 **Flowers** 1938

below left
19 **Nude (back view)** 1926

below right
20 **Figure Study (Artist's Wife)** 1931

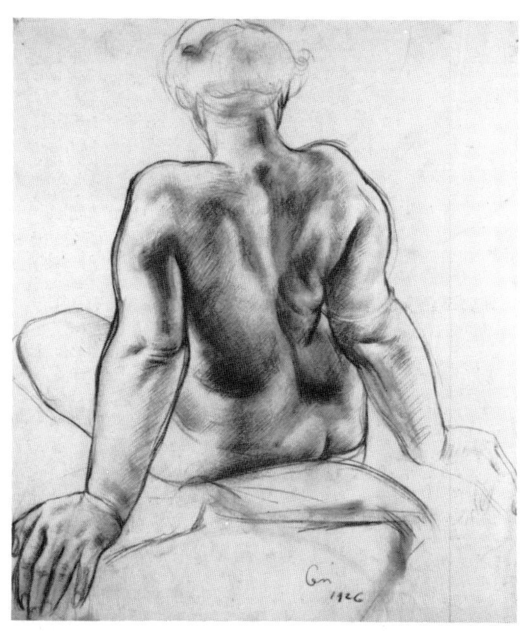

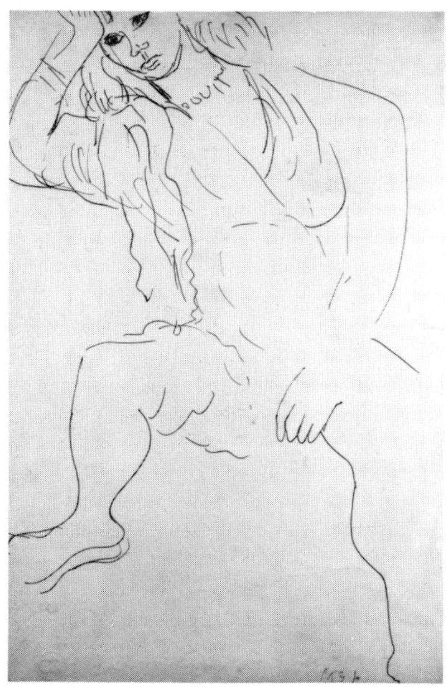

21 **Portrait of the Artist's Wife, Sleeping** 1932

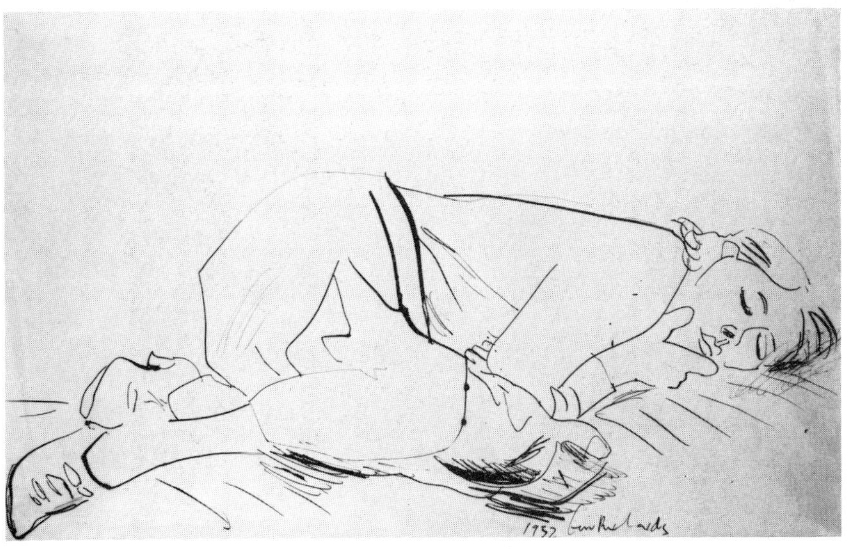

28 **Study for a Relief Construction** 1936

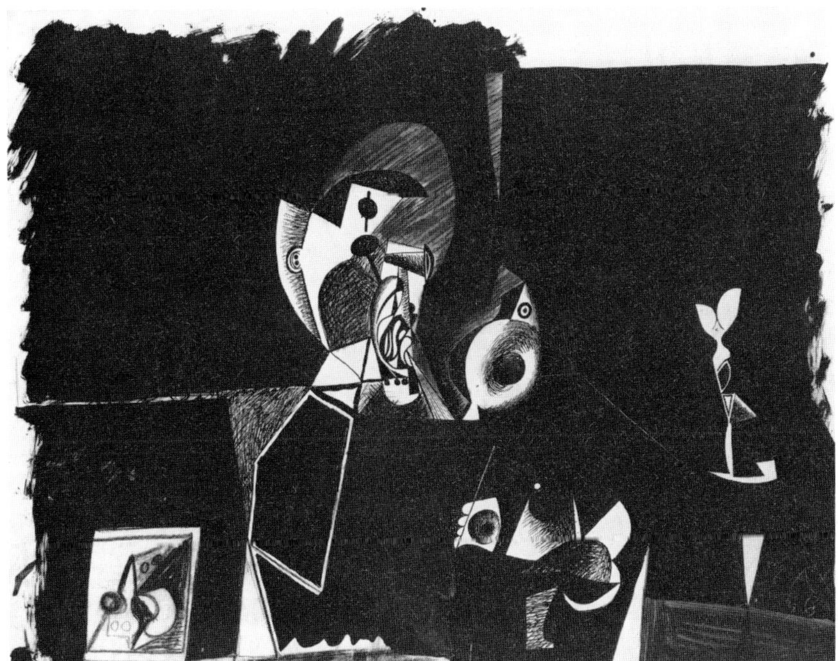

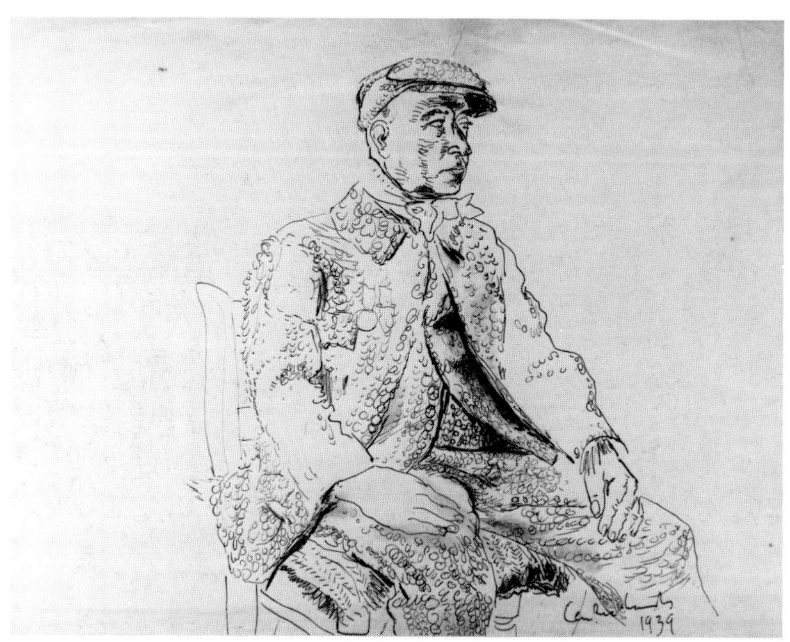

32 Portrait of Bert Matthews,
    Pearly King of
    Hampstead 1939

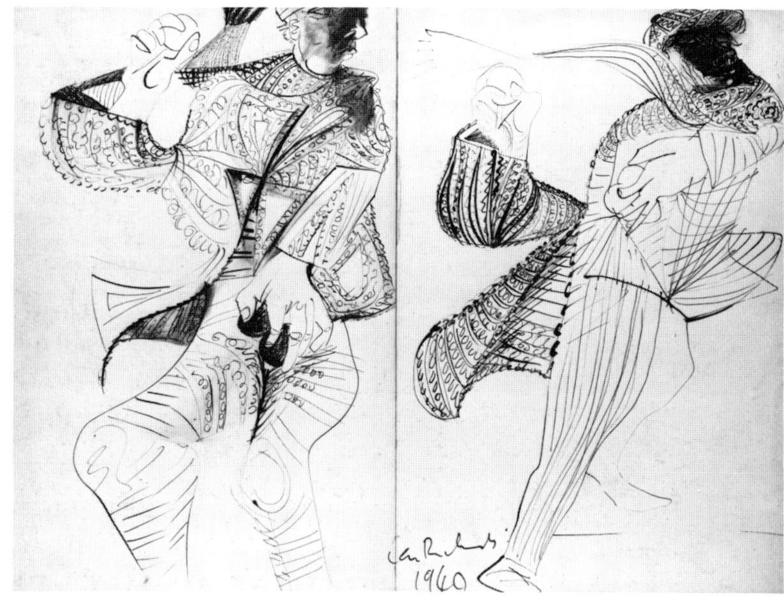

33 Coconut Shy (two studies)
    1940

36 Welsh Coastline
('Rocks') 1942

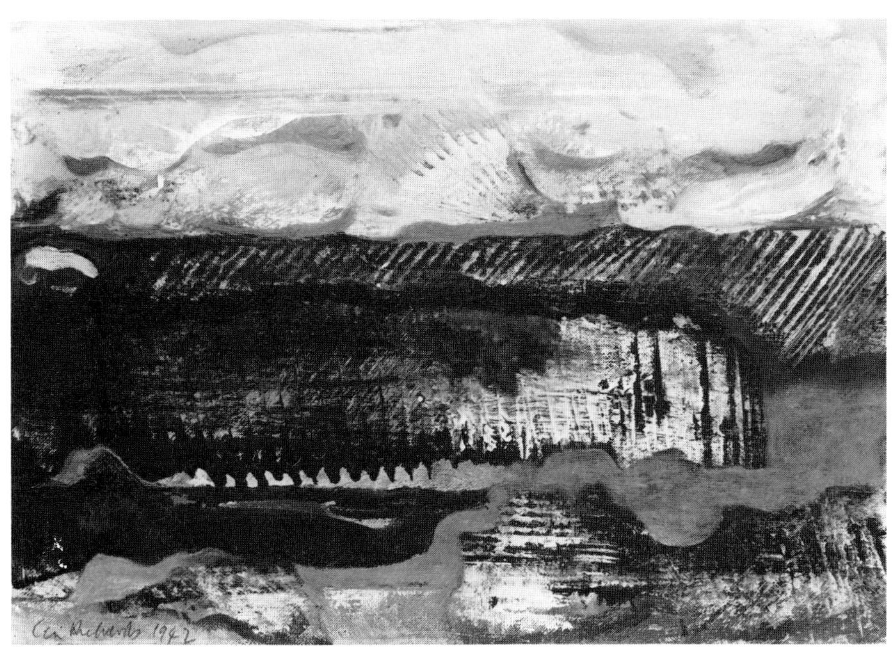

39 Cycle of Nature 1944

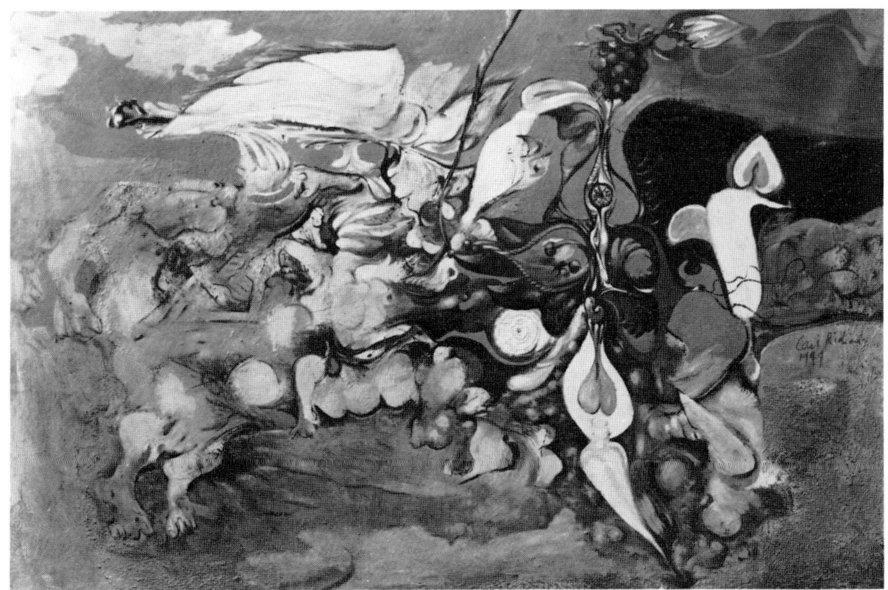

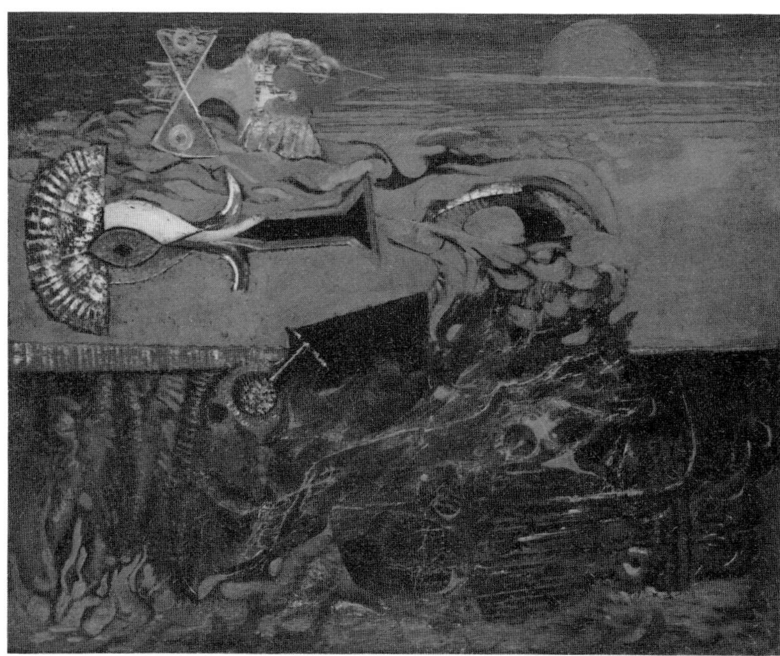

41 **Falling Forms** 1944

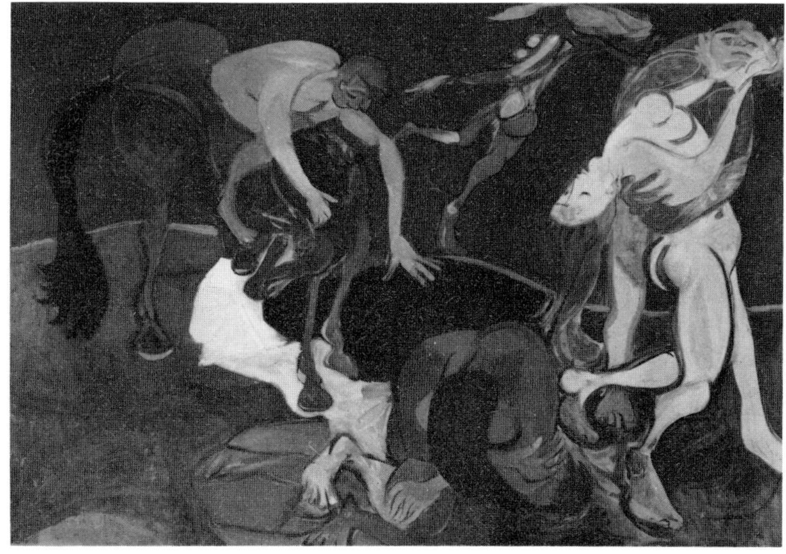

44 **The Rape of the
Sabines** 1948

47 **Interior with Piano, Woman and Child Painting** 1949

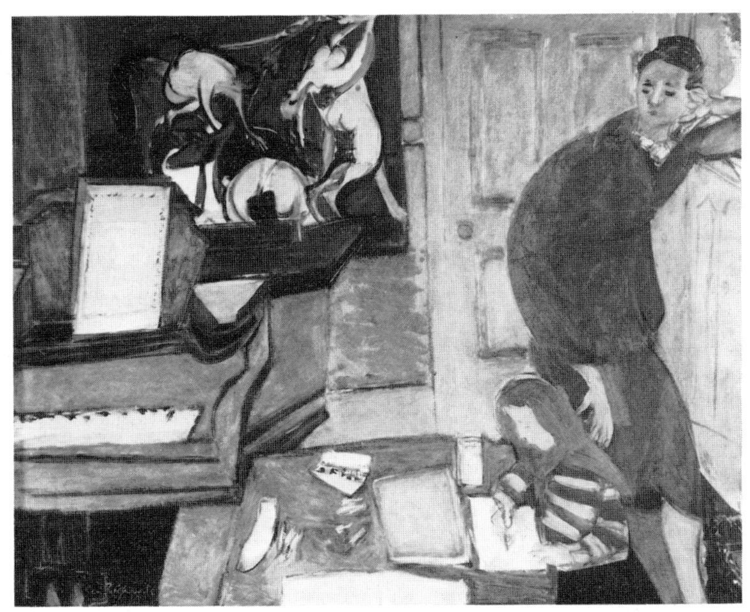

50 **Yellow Interior** 1950

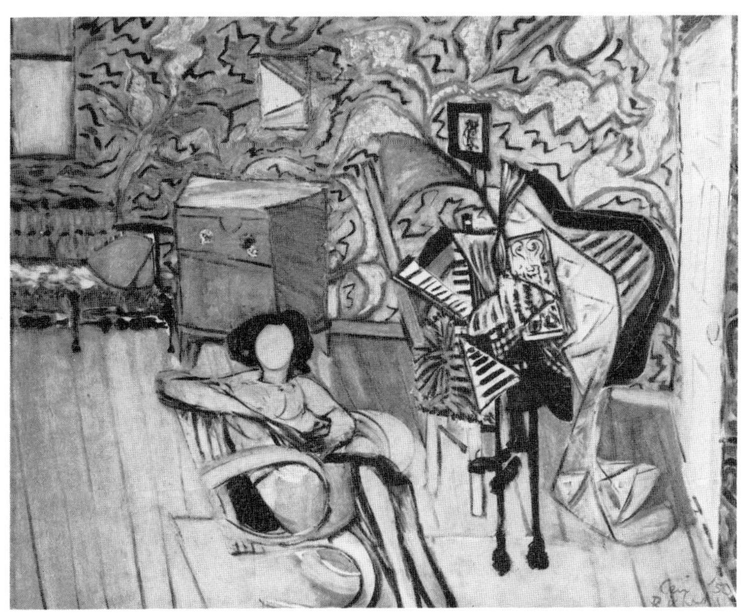

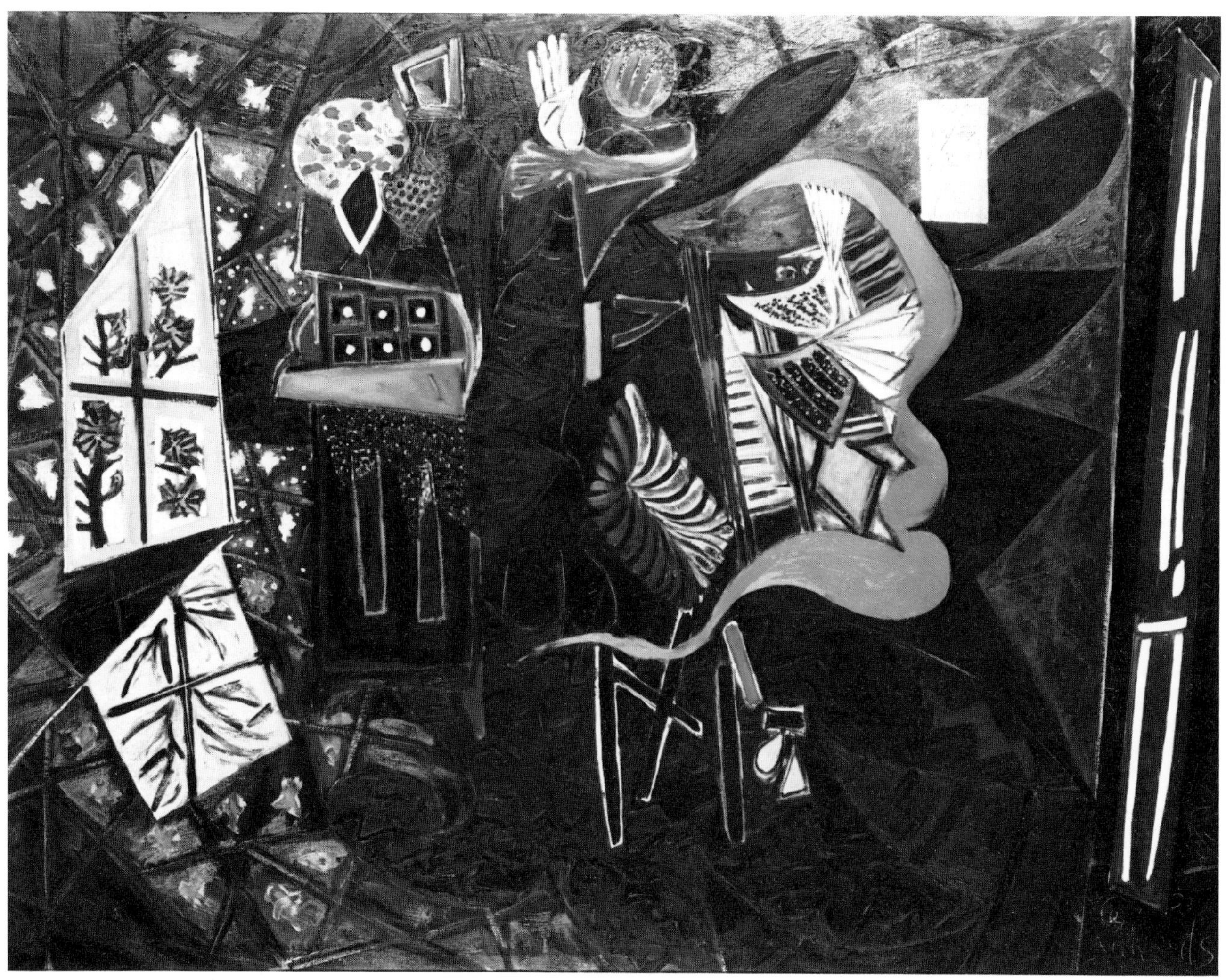

51 **Cold Light, Deep Shadow** 1950

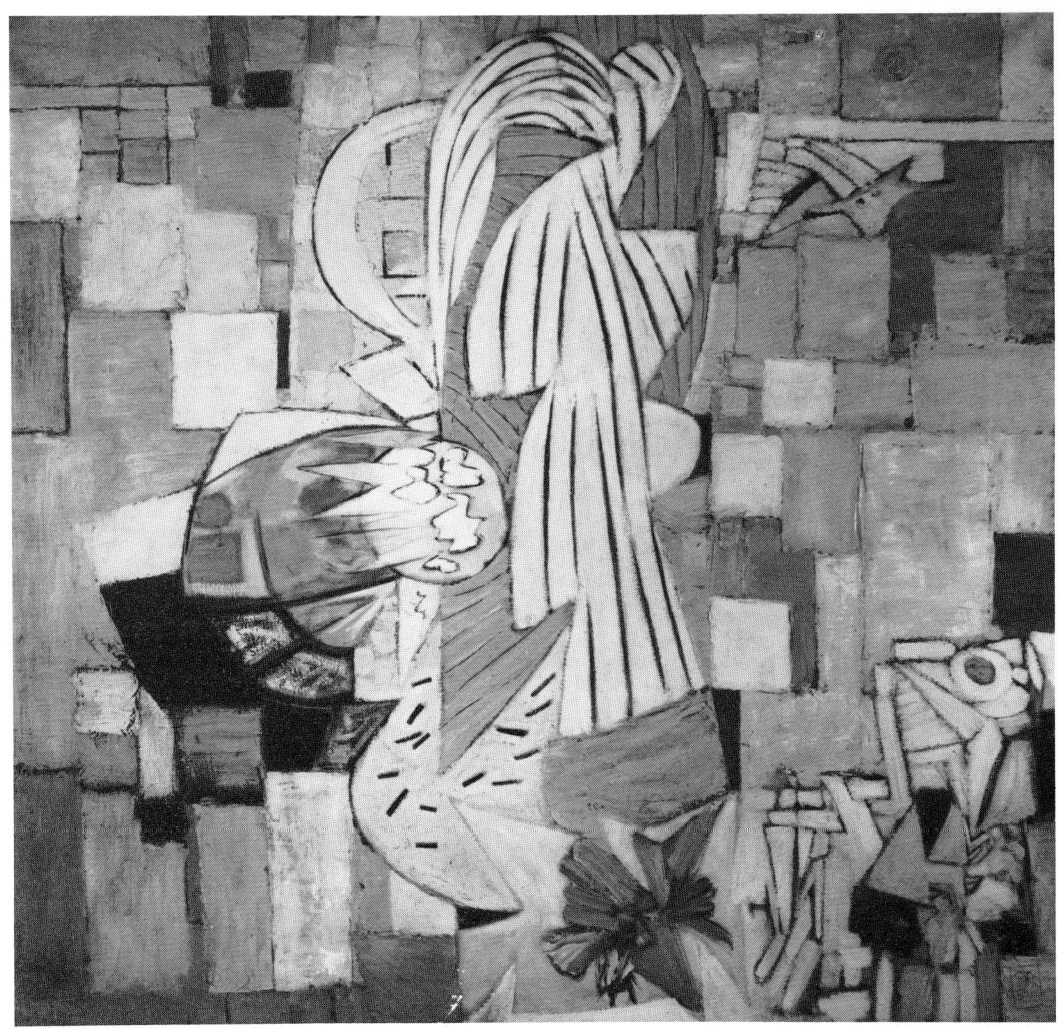

56 **Trafalgar Square** 1951

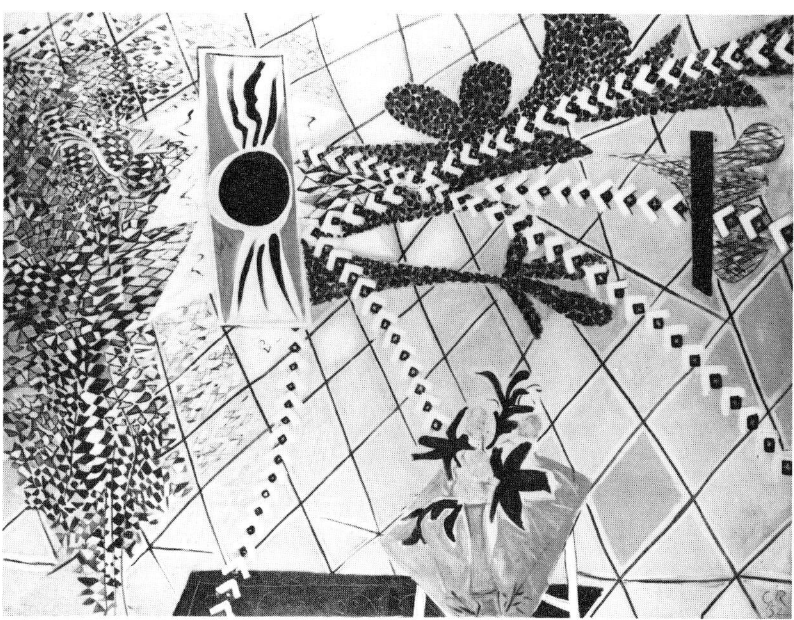

58 Sunlight in a Room 1952

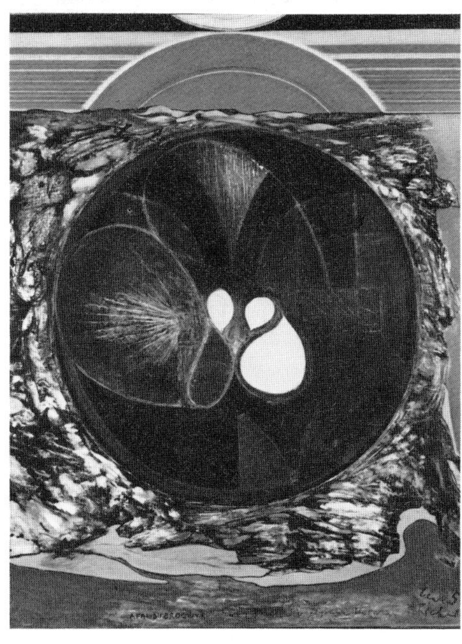

60 The Black Apple of Gower
    (Afal du Brogwyr) 1952

[46]

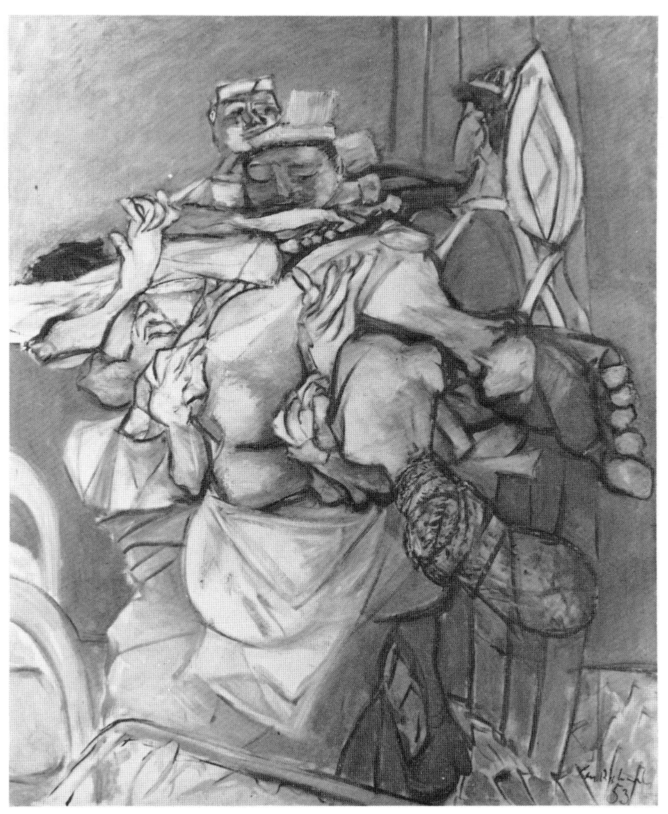

64 **The Return of the Patient**
(**The Unconscious Man**) 1953

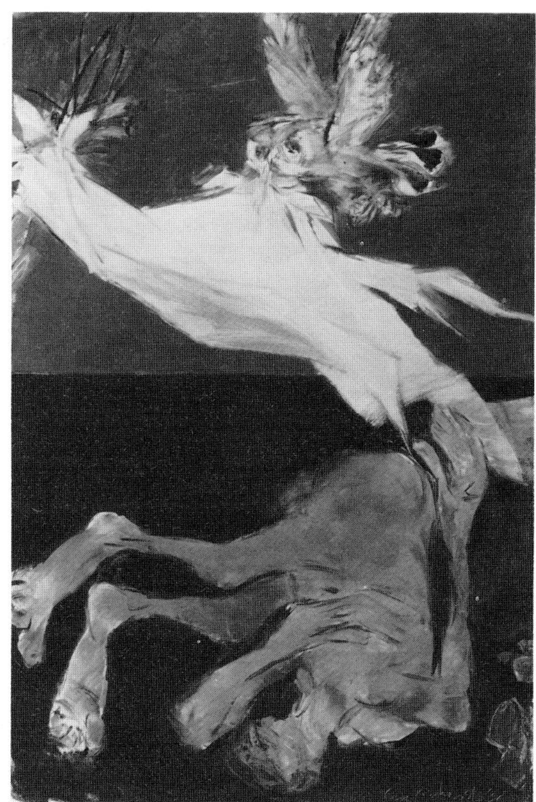

67 **'Do not go gentle into that
good night'** 1956

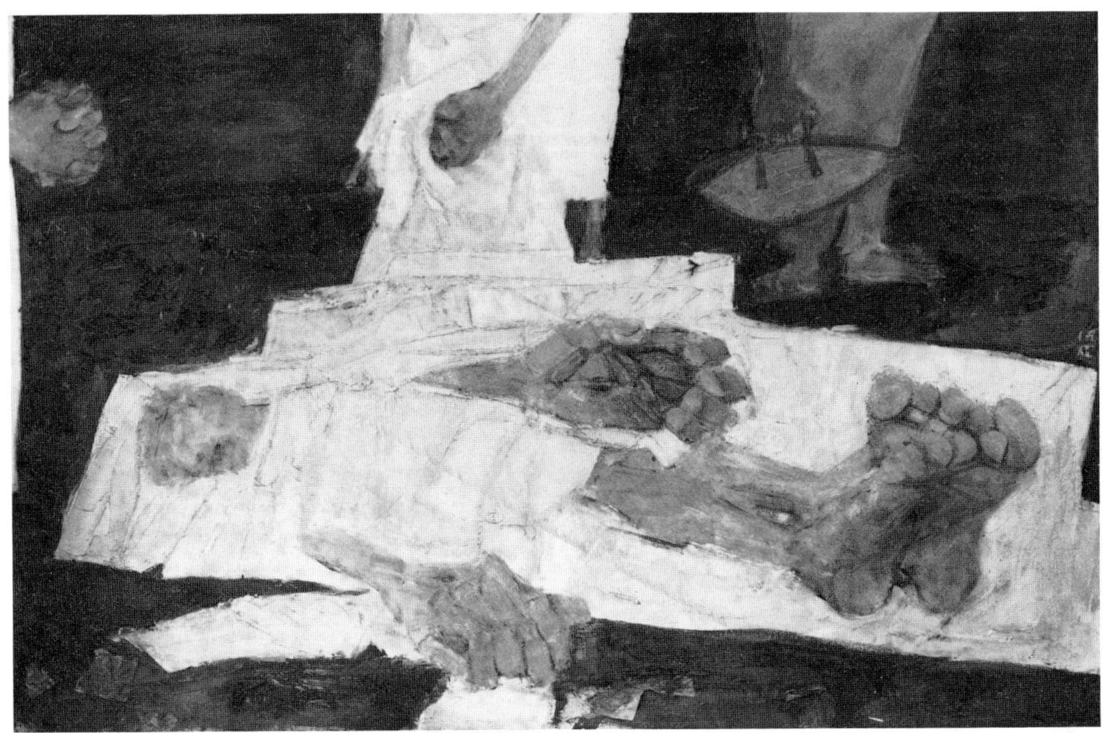

69 The Deposition 1958

70 La Cathédrale Engloutie
(Arabesque 1) 1959

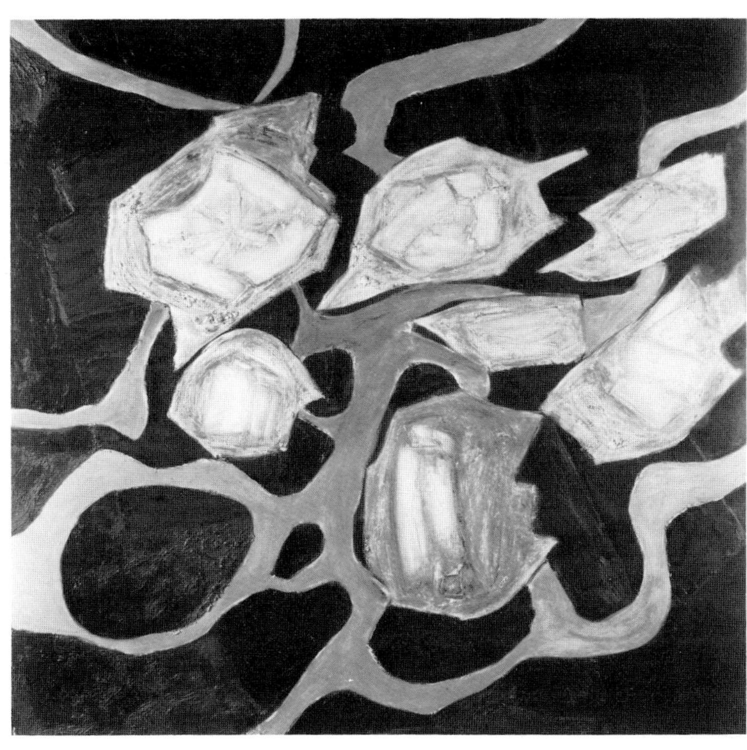

73 La Cathédrale Engloutie
(augmentez progressivement)
1960–61

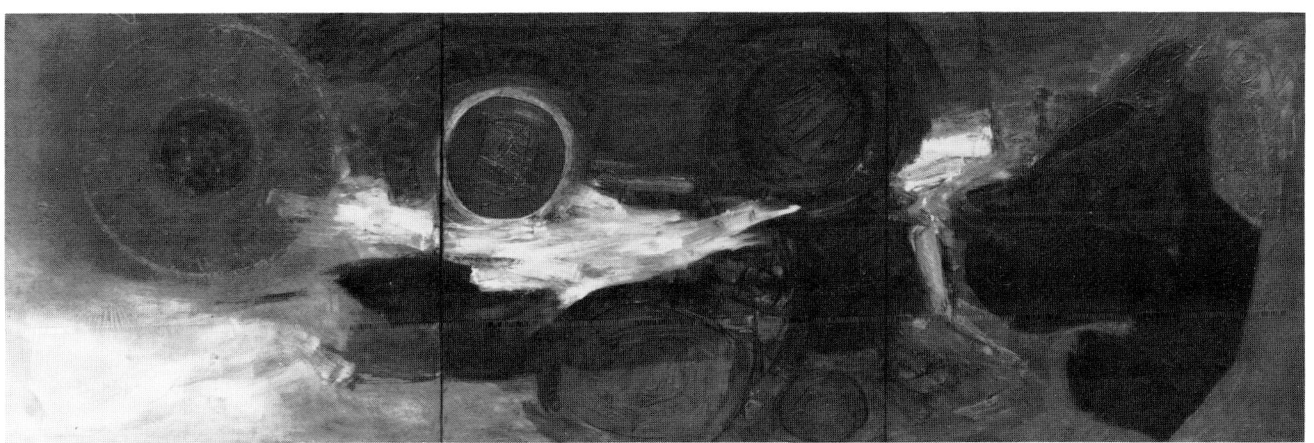

[49]

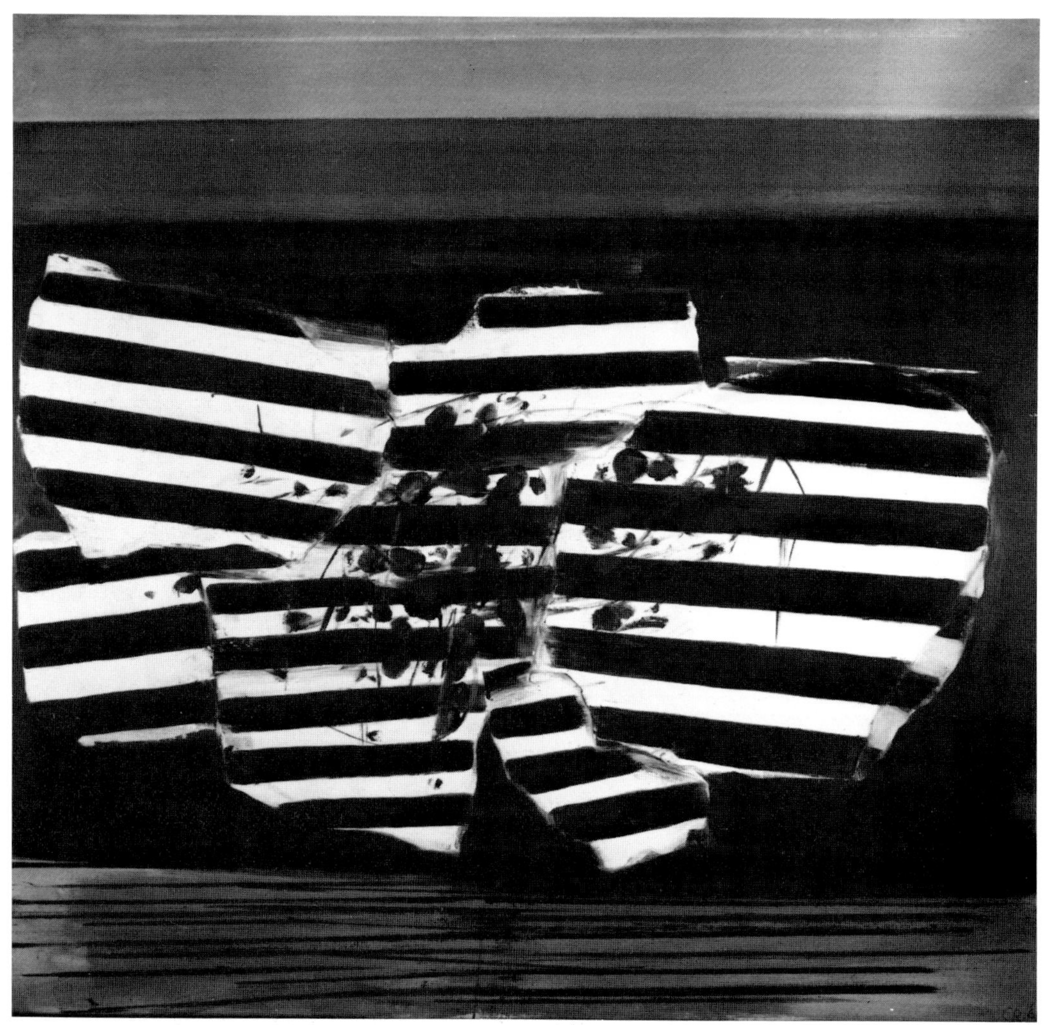

75 **La Cathédrale Engloutie**
   (Jeux de vagues) 1961

[50]

80 La Cathédrale Engloutie
(Blue Swirl) 1960

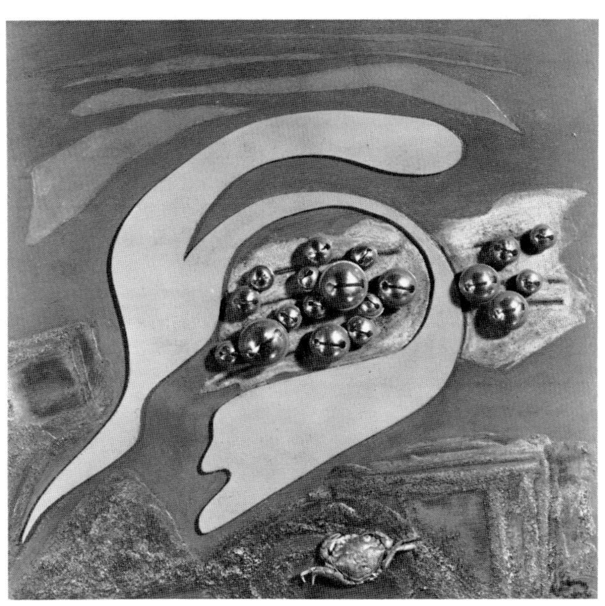

81 La Cathédrale Engloutie
1960

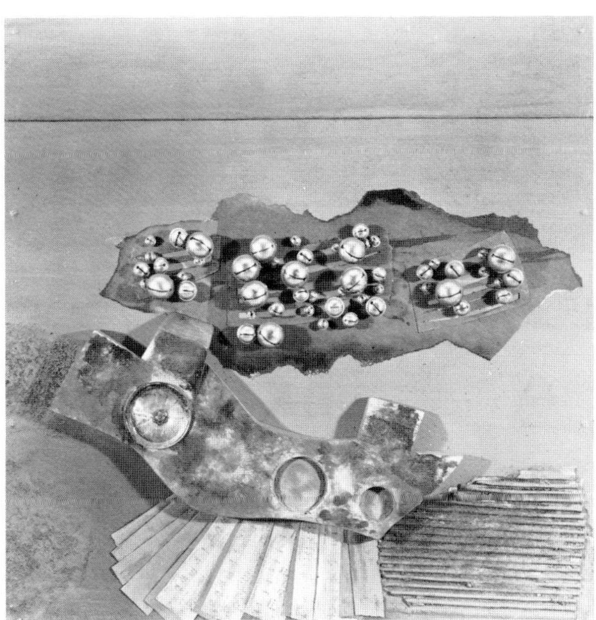

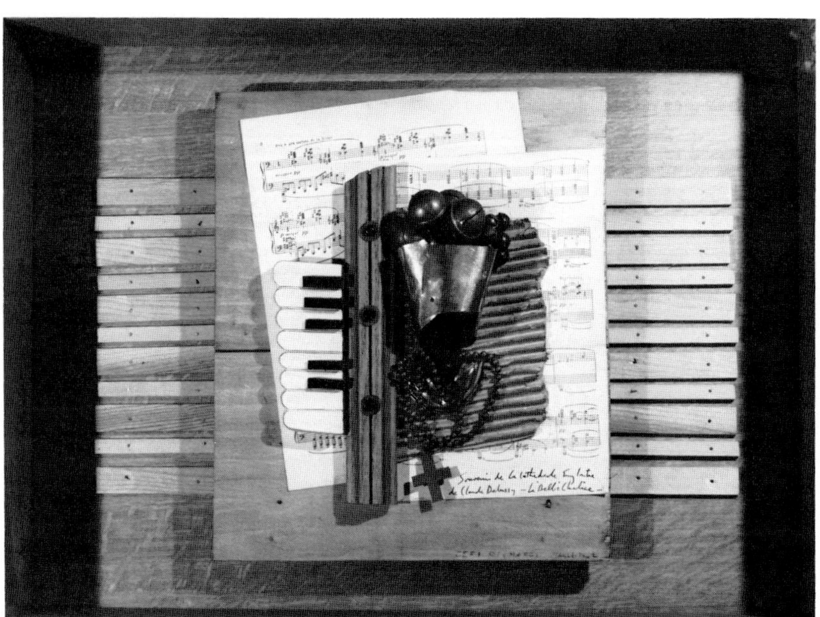

83 La Cathédrale Engloutie
(La Belle Chalice) 1962

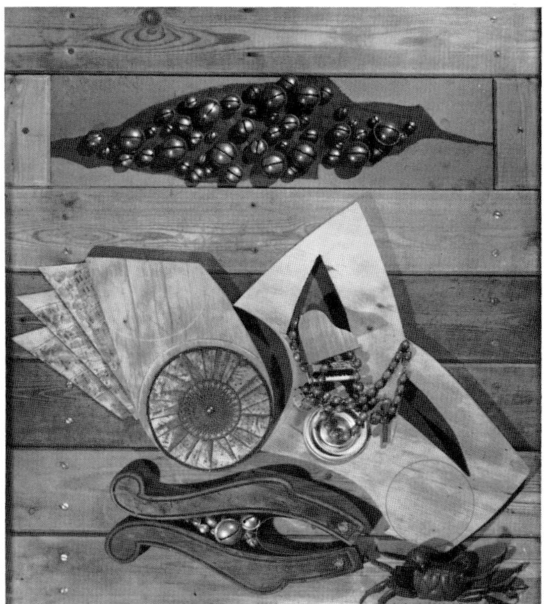

84 Souvenir de la Cathédrale
Engloutie 1960–62

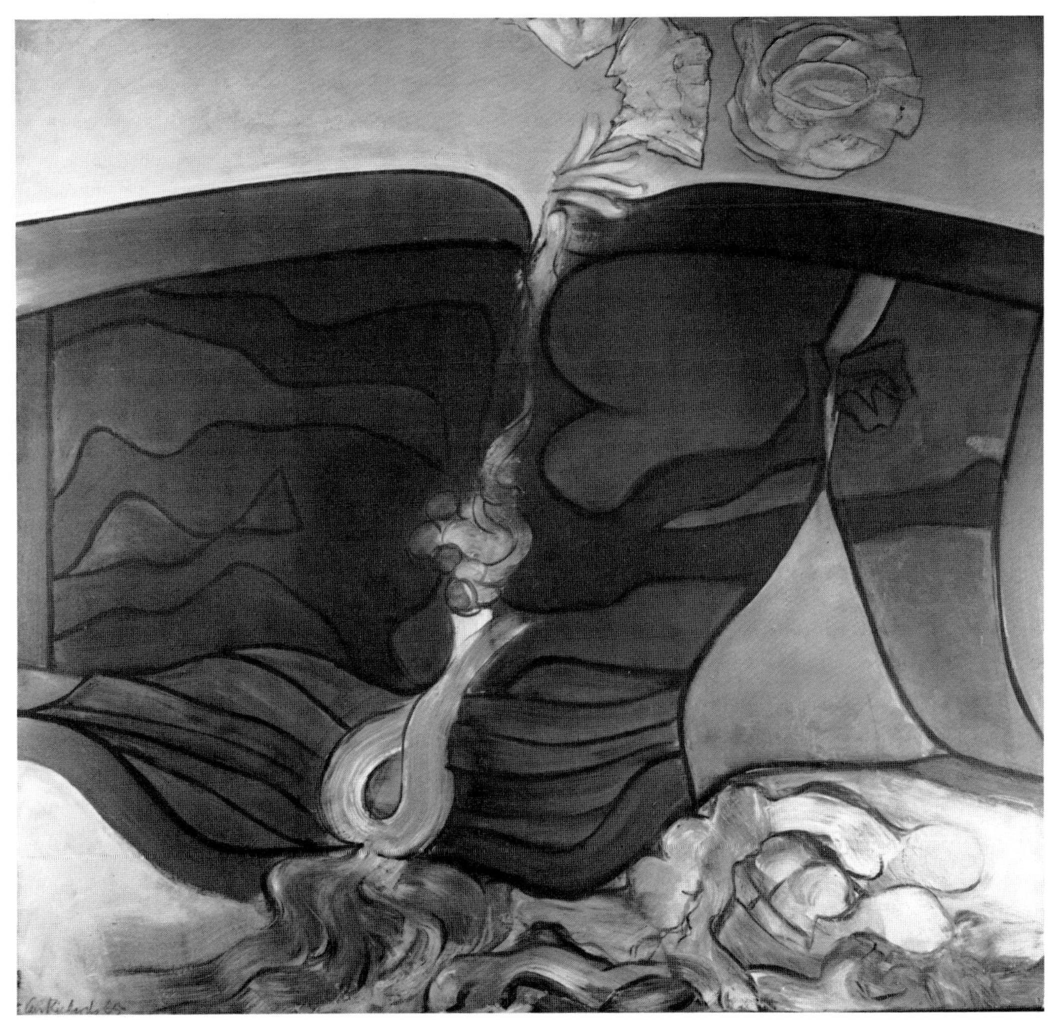

86 'The force that through the
green fuse' 1965

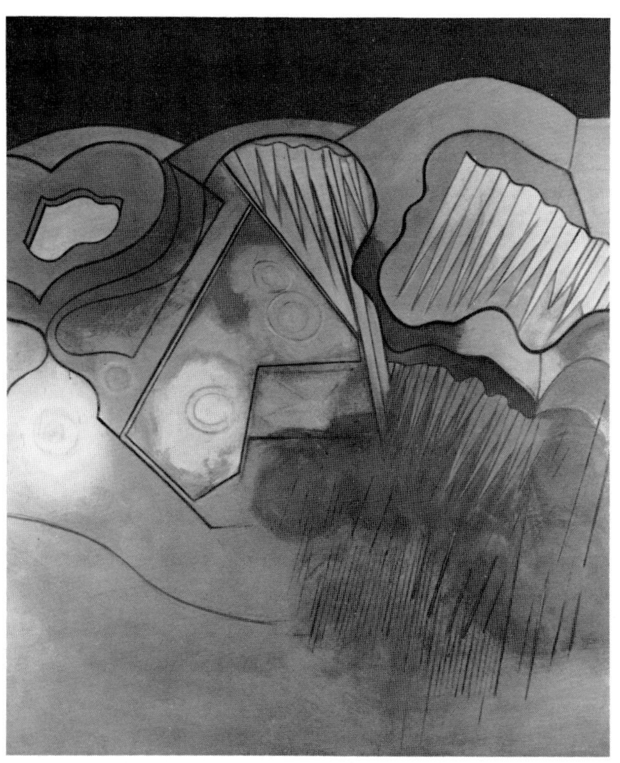

87 Jardins sous la pluie 1967

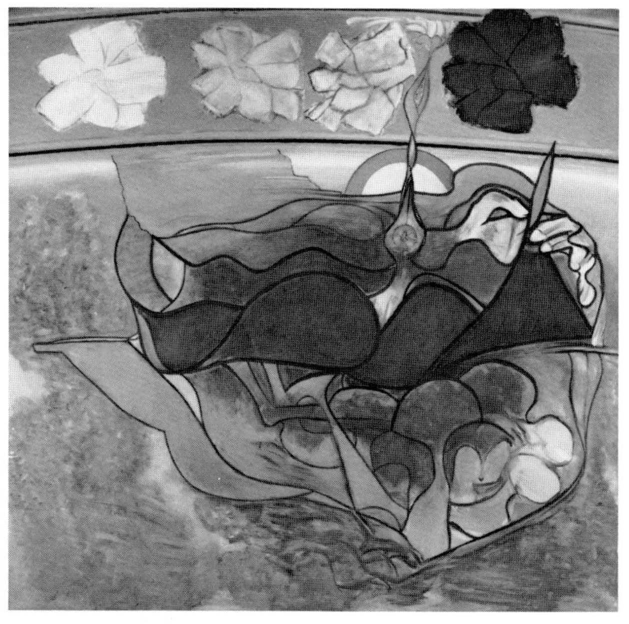

92 Summer 1968

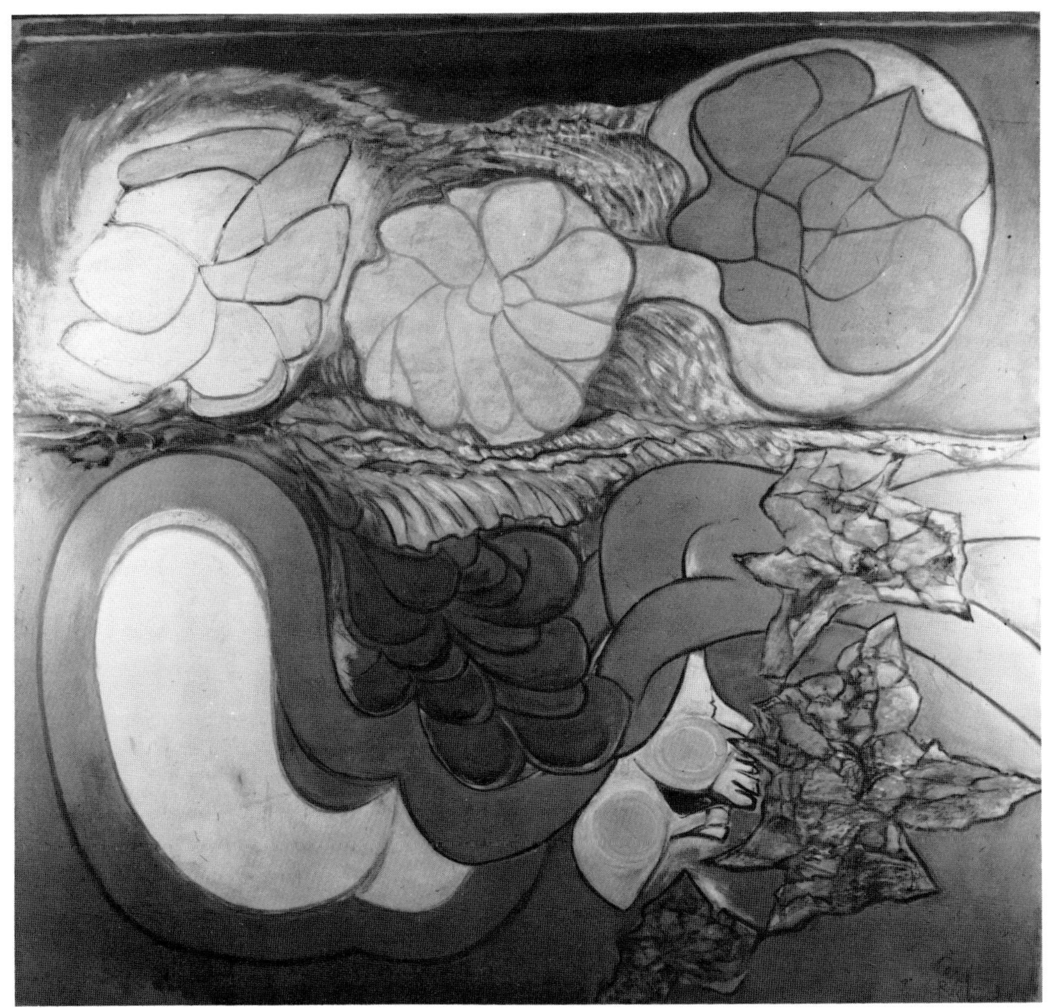

93 **The Seasons** 1964–69

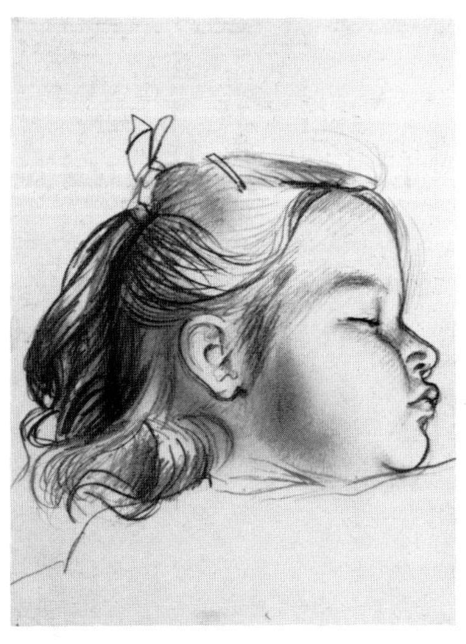

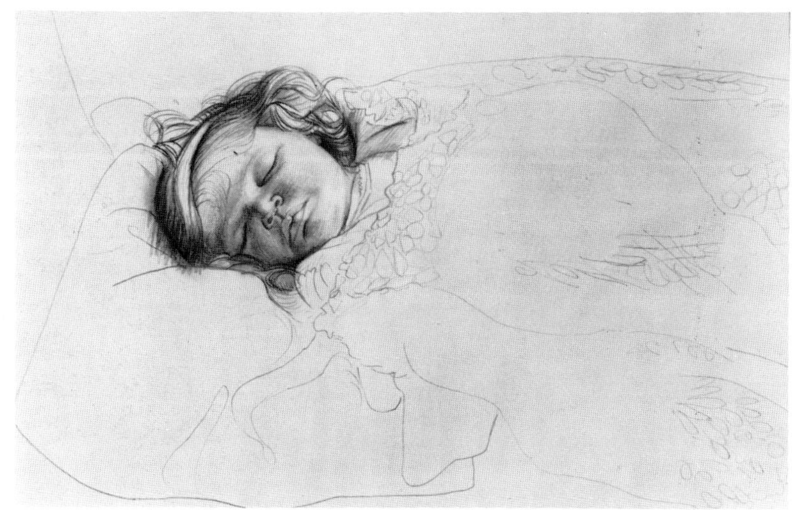

VIII The Artist's Father
in Bed 1957

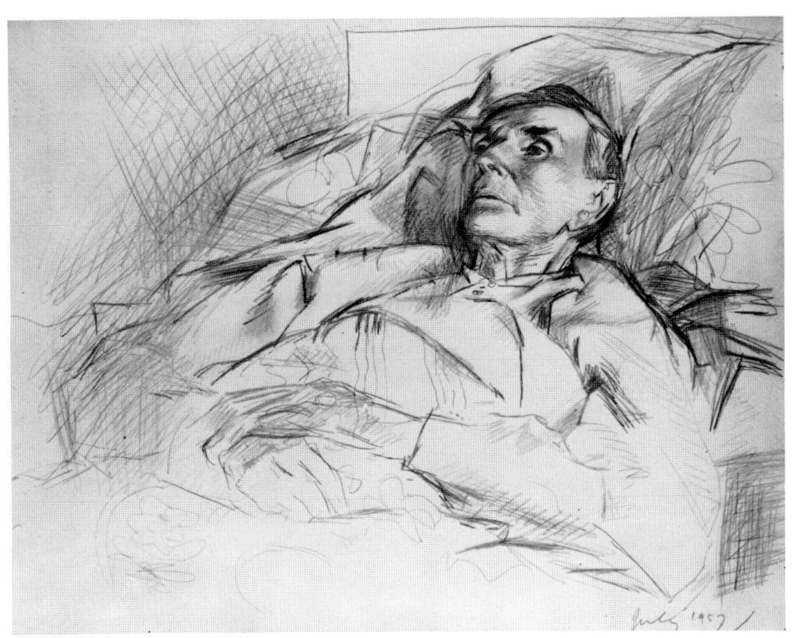

IX Portrait of the Artist's
Daughter: Rachel
writing 1957

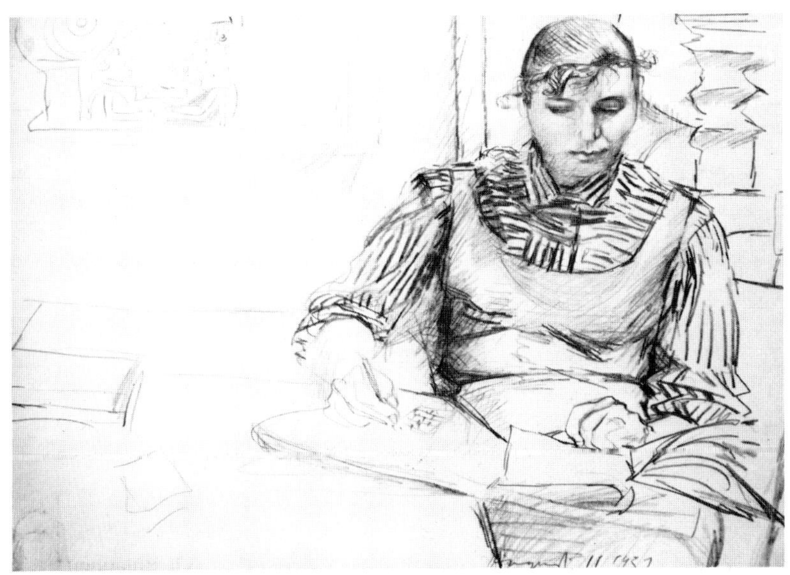

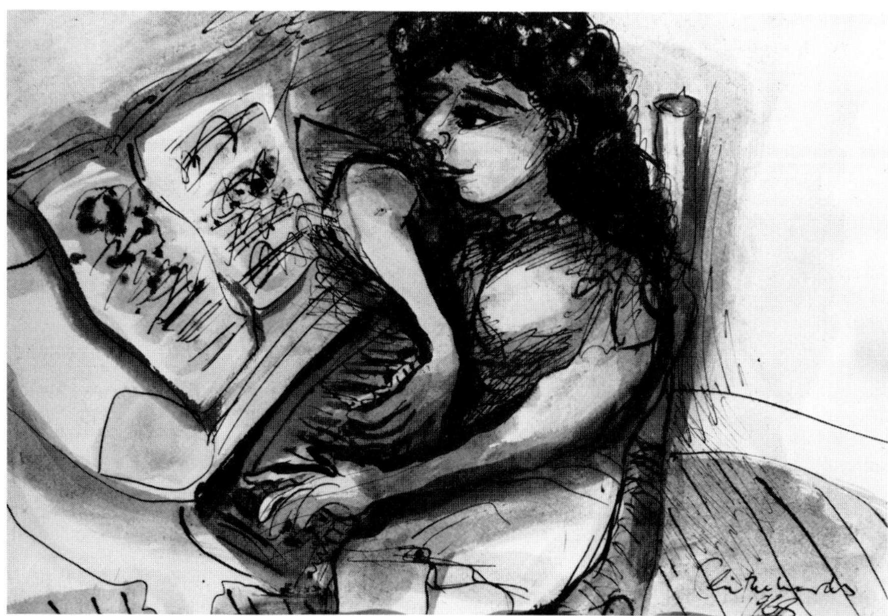

XI Pianist 1968

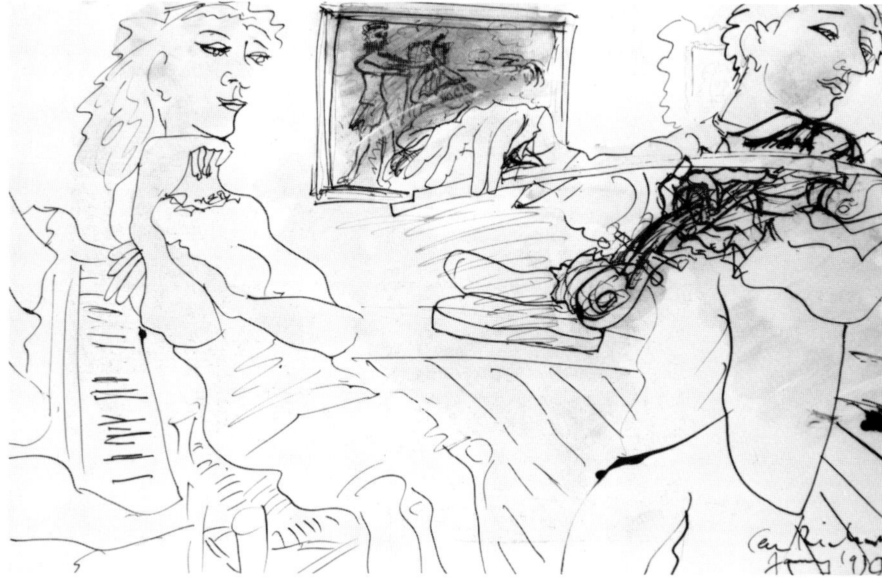

XIV Two Musicians 1970

[58]

XVII Five studies for
lithographs on
Dylan Thomas
themes 1945

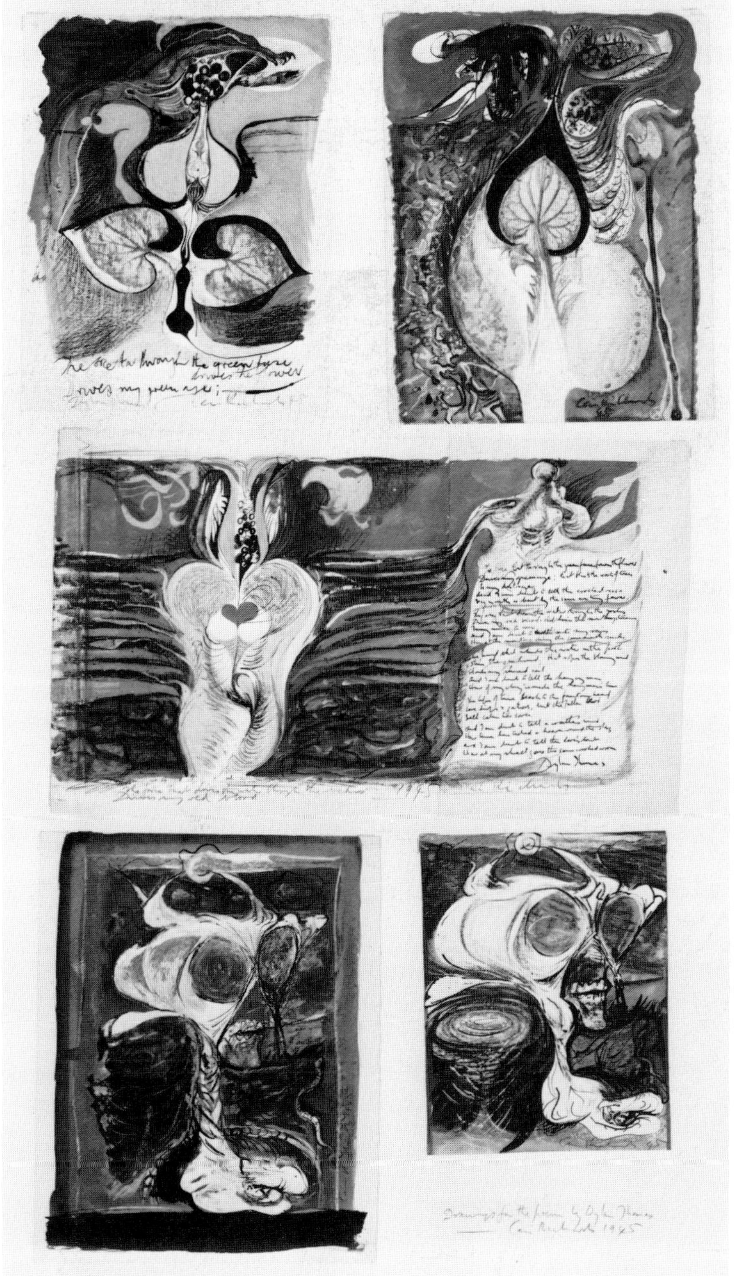

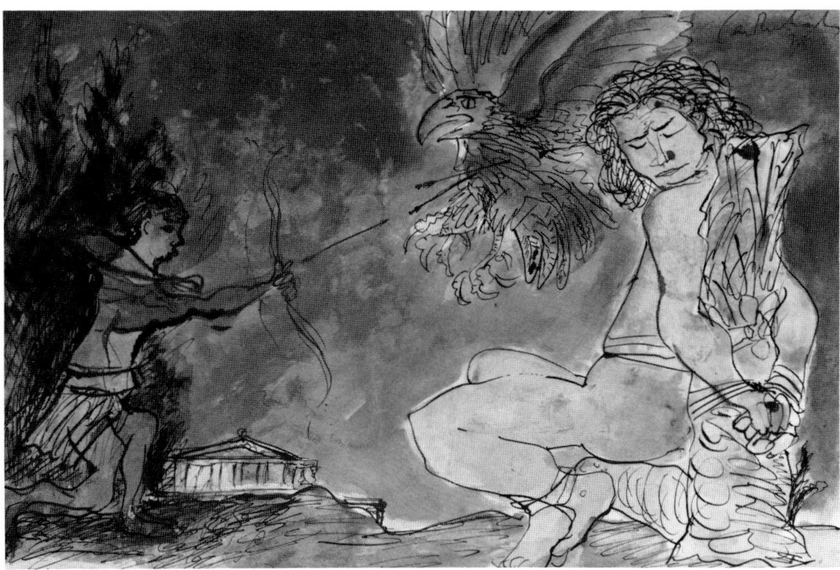

XVIII Prometheus 1970

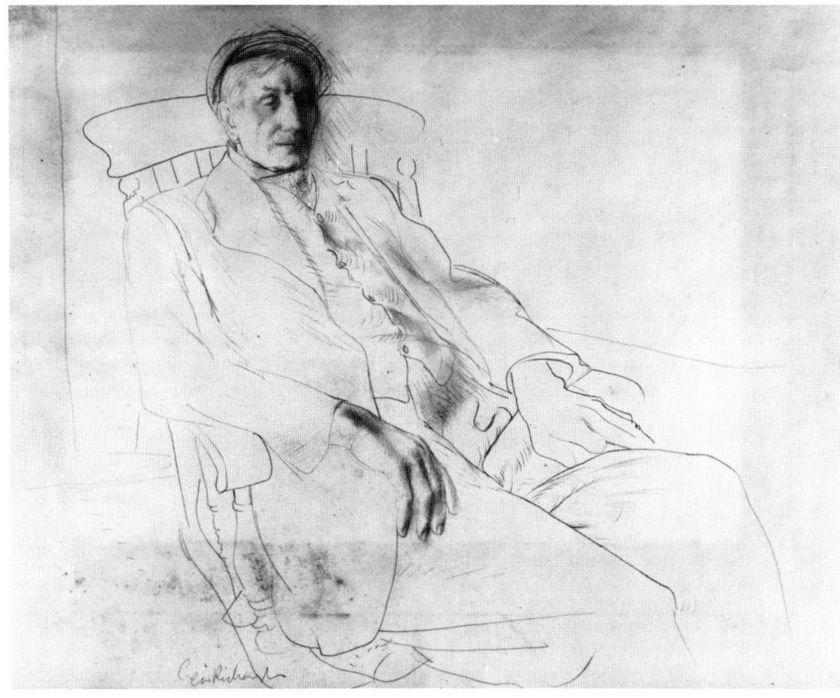

XIX The Artist's Father 1942

Catalogue

Dimensions are given in centimetres followed by inches in brackets; height precedes width

CONSTRUCTIONS 1930s

1 **Piano** 1934
Signed on back
Relief construction, wood, metal, sand on painted wood
23 × 28 (9 × 11)
Portsmouth City Museum and Art Gallery

2 **Man with a Pipe** 1934
Relief construction, wood, oil, paper collage on wood
45 × 41 (17¾ × 16)
Private collection

3 **Relief Construction with Fragment of Music** 1934
Relief construction, wood, metal, paper collage on wood
18.5 × 28 (7¼ × 11)
Glynn Vivian Art Gallery & Museum, Swansea

4 **Head** 1935
Signed and dated 'CR 35' lower R
Relief construction, wood and painted collage on painted wood
60 × 62.5 (23½ × 24½)
Frances Richards

5 **White and Dark** 1936
Signed and dated 'CR 36' lower R
Relief construction, wood on painted wood
50 × 54 (19¾ × 21¼)
National Museum of Wales, Cardiff

6 **The Sculptor and his Model** 1936
Signed and dated 'CR 1936' lower L
Relief construction, wood and metal on painted wood
103.5 × 85.5 (40½ × 33¾)
Frances Richards

7 **The Sculptor and his Studio** 1937
Inscribed, signed and dated 'The Sculptor in his Studio Ceri Richards 1937' on back
Wood relief with paper collage, ink and pencil, strip brass and nails
46.5 × 43 (18¼ × 17)
Tate Gallery (T308)

8 **Two Females** 1937/8
Signed and dated 'Ceri Richards 37' lower R.
Inscribed, signed and dated 'Ceri Richards, 26 St Peter's Square, Hammersmith W.6 Two Females 1937–38' on back
Painted wooden relief construction with strip brass and two brass ornaments nailed on
160 × 117 (63 × 46)
Tate Gallery (T307)

9 **Mother and Child** 1938
Dated lower L
Relief construction, wood on painted wood
84 × 66 (33 × 26)
Fischer Fine Art, London

10 **The Variable Costerwoman** 1938
Inscribed and dated 'The Variable Costerwoman '38' lower R
Relief construction, wood, metal, mixed media on painted wood
84 × 81.3 (33 × 32)
City of Manchester Art Galleries

PAINTINGS 1930s

11 **Portrait of the Artist's Sister** 1932
Oil on canvas
71 × 55.6 (28 × 22)
Frances Richards

12 **Reclining Nude** 1932
Signed and dated 'Ceri Richards 1932' top R
Oil on canvas
89 × 107 (35 × 42)
Frances Richards

13 **Still Life with Violin** 1934
Signed and dated 'Ceri Richards 26 St Peter's Square, Hammersmith W.6' on back
Oil on canvas
63.5 × 76 (25 × 30)
Frances Richards

14 **The Artist and his Model** 1937
Signed and dated 'Ceri

Richards 1937' lower L
Oil on canvas
107 × 89 (42 × 35)
Frances Richards

**15 The Female Contains All
Qualities** 1938
Signed and dated 'Ceri
Richards 1937' lower L.
Inscribed 'The Female unites
all qualities/Ceri Richards
1937' on back
Oil on canvas
107 × 89 (42 × 35)
Tate Gallery (T798)

16 Flowers 1938
Signed and dated 'Ceri
Richards 1938' lower R
Oil on canvas
89 × 107 (35 × 42)
Frances Richards

17 Chimera Costerwoman 1939
Signed and dated 'Ceri
Richards 1939' lower R
Oil on canvas
101.5 × 45.5 (40 × 18)
Frances Richards

18 Costerwoman 1939
Signed and dated 'Ceri
Richards 1939' lower L
Oil on canvas
76 × 63.5 (30 × 25)
*Glynn Vivian Art Gallery &
Museum, Swansea*

DRAWINGS 1930s

19 Nude (back view) 1926
Signed 'Ceri 1926' lower R
Red chalk on paper
41.5 × 34.5 ($16\frac{1}{4}$ × $13\frac{1}{2}$)
Frances Richards

**20 Figure Study (Artist's
wife)** 1931
Dated '1931' lower R,
embossed (studio stamp) 'CR'
lower L
Pen and ink on paper
49 × 31 ($19\frac{1}{2}$ × $12\frac{1}{4}$)
Frances Richards

**21 Portrait of the Artist's Wife,
Sleeping** 1932
Signed and dated '1932 Ceri
Richards' lower R
Pen and ink on paper
28 × 45.5 (11 × 18)
Frances Richards

**22 Study for Relief
Construction** 1934
Signed and dated 'Ceri
Richards 1934'
Pen and ink and wash
on paper
18.7 × 44.8 ($7\frac{3}{8}$ × $17\frac{5}{8}$)
Frances Richards

**23 Study for Relief
Construction** 1934
Signed and dated 'Ceri
Richards 1934' lower R
Pen and ink and wash
on paper
28 × 45 (11 × $17\frac{3}{4}$)
Frances Richards

24 The Sculptor 1934
Signed and dated 'Ceri
Richards 1934' lower R
Pen and ink and wash
on paper
30.7 × 44.5 (12 × $17\frac{1}{2}$)
Frances Richards

**25 Studies for Relief
Construction** 1936
Signed and dated 'Ceri
Richards 1936' lower L
Pen and ink, pencil,

crayon on paper
31.5 × 40.5 ($12\frac{3}{8}$ × 16)
Frances Richards

26 Studies for Sculpture 1936
Signed and dated 'Ceri
Richards 1936' lower R
Pen and ink and wash
on paper
27.5 × 37.3 ($10\frac{3}{4}$ × $14\frac{5}{8}$)
Frances Richards

27 Drawing 1936
Signed and dated 'Ceri
Richards 1936' lower R
Pen and wash on paper
45.6 × 58.5 ($17\frac{1}{4}$ × 23)
Tate Gallery (2040)

**28 Study for a Relief
Construction** 1936
Signed 'CR 36' lower R
Pen and brush with conté
crayon on paper
45.6 × 58.4 (18 × 23)
Tate Gallery (2041)

**29 The Sculptor and the
Model** 1936
Embossed (studio stamp) 'CR'
lower L
Pen and ink, watercolour,
chalk on paper
30.7 × 24 (12 × $9\frac{1}{2}$)
Frances Richards

**30 Study for Relief Construction
(two females)** c.1937
Pen and ink, pencil on paper
22.2 × 16.5 ($8\frac{3}{4}$ × $6\frac{1}{2}$)
Frances Richards

31 Pearly King and Queen 1939
Signed and dated 'Ceri
Richards 1939' lower R
Pen and ink on paper
30 × 37 ($11\frac{3}{4}$ × $14\frac{1}{2}$)
Frances Richards

32 **Portrait of Bert Matthews, Pearly King of Hampstead** 1939
Signed and dated 'Ceri Richards 1939' lower R
Pen and ink on paper
40 × 49.5 ($15\frac{3}{4}$ × $19\frac{1}{2}$)
Frances Richards

33 **Coconut Shy (two studies)** 1940
Signed and dated 'Ceri Richards 1940' lower centre
Pen and ink on paper
38 × 49.5 (15 × $19\frac{1}{2}$)
Frances Richards

PAINTINGS 1940s (wartime)

34 **Blossoms** 1940
Signed and dated 'Ceri Richards 1940' lower R.
Inscribed 'Ceri Richards 'Blossoms' 1940' along strip of folded canvas at bottom.
Signed 'Ceri Richards' on back.
Oil on canvas
51 × 61 (20 × 24)
Tate Gallery (5354)

35 **Pianist** 1940
Signed and dated 'Ceri Richards 1940' lower R
Oil on wood panel
51 × 69 (20 × 27)
F.E. McWilliam

36 **Welsh Coastline (Rocks)** 1942
Signed and dated
Oil on canvas
25.4 × 35.6 (10 × 14)
National Museum of Wales, Cardiff

37 **Rocks** 1942
Oil on canvas
65 × 77 ($24\frac{1}{2}$ × $30\frac{1}{4}$)
Arts Council of Great Britain

38 **The Sculptor's Landscape (Homage to Henry Moore)** 1943
Signed and dated lower L
Oil on canvas
87 × 105 ($34\frac{1}{2}$ × $41\frac{1}{2}$)
Glynn Vivian Art Gallery & Museum, Swansea

39 **Cycle of Nature** 1944
Signed and dated 'Ceri Richards 1944' centre R
Oil on canvas
101 × 154.4 (40 × 60)
National Museum of Wales, Cardiff

40 **'The force that drives the water through the rock drives my red blood'** 1943/4
Signed and dated 'Ceri Richards 1943–4' lower L
Oil on canvas
107 × 89 (42 × 35)
Mr and Mrs Eugene Rosenberg

41 **Falling Forms** 1944
Signed and dated 'Ceri Richards 1944' lower R
Oil on canvas
51 × 61 (20 × 24)
Private Collection

42 **'The force that through the green fuse drives the flower' (Cycle of Nature)** 1945
Signed and dated lower L
Oil on canvas
87 × 105 ($34\frac{1}{2}$ × $41\frac{1}{2}$)
Private Collection

PAINTINGS (later 40s/early 50s)

43 **Coconut Shy** 1948
Signed and dated 'Ceri Richards '48' lower L
Oil on canvas
63 × 76 (25 × 30)
Mrs Rachel Patterson

44 **The Rape of the Sabines** 1948
Signed and dated 'Ceri Richards 1948' lower L
Oil on canvas
96.5 × 142.5 (38 × 56)
Estate of the artist

45 **Red Interior with Music by Albeniz** 1949
Signed and dated 'Ceri Richards Aug 49' lower L
Oil on canvas
101.5 × 101.5 (40 × 40)
Frances Richards

46 **Blue Interior with Dice** 1949
Oil on canvas
101.5 × 127 (40 × 50)
Arts Council of Great Britain

47 **Interior with Piano, Woman and Child Painting** 1949
Signed and dated 'Ceri Richards 1949'
Oil on canvas
96.5 × 124.5 (38 × 49)
Mr and Mrs Wilfrid Giardelli

48 **Tulips** 1949
Signed and dated 'Ceri Richards 1949' lower R
Oil on canvas
91.5 × 106.5 (36 × 42)
University College of Wales (Neuadd Pantycelyn)

49 St Cecilia 1949
Signed and dated 'Ceri
Richards 49' lower R
Oil on canvas
77 × 94.5 (30½ × 37¼)
Bassetlaw District Council

50 Yellow Interior 1950
Signed and dated 'Ceri
Richards 1950'
Oil on canvas
81.5 × 101.5 (32 × 40)
Mr and Mrs Wilfrid Giardelli

**51 Cold Light, Deep
Shadow** 1950
Signed and dated 'Ceri
50/Richards' lower R
Oil on canvas
91.5 × 116.5 (36 × 46)
Tate Gallery (5949)

**52 Light Interior (Music
Room)** 1950
Signed and dated 'Ceri
Richards 50' lower R
Oil on canvas
101.5 × 91.5 (40 × 36)
Arthur Giardelli

53 Shadows in a Room 1950
Signed and dated 'Ceri
Richards '50' lower R
Oil on canvas
91.5 × 114 (36 × 45)
Private Collection

54 Trafalgar Square 1950
Signed and dated ''50 Ceri
Richards' lower R. Inscribed
'Trafalgar Square/Richards'
on back
Oil on canvas
151 × 244 (60 × 96)
Tate Gallery (T292)

**55 Trafalgar Square (Version
II)** 1951
Oil on canvas
114 × 151 (44 × 59½)
Walker Art Gallery, Liverpool

56 Trafalgar Square 1951
Signed and dated 'CR '51', in
pencil lower R
Oil on canvas
91.5 × 91.5 (36 × 36)
Mel & Rhiannon Gooding

57 Trafalgar Square 1951–53
Signed and dated on back
Oil on canvas
81 × 99 (32 × 39)
Mrs Rachel Patterson

58 Sunlight in a Room 1952
Signed and dated 'CR '52'
lower R
Oil on canvas
114.5 × 152 (45 × 60)
Mel & Rhiannon Gooding

59 Sunlight and Shadow 1952
Dated ''52' lower R
Oil on canvas
90 × 90 (35½ × 35½)
Mrs Rachel Patterson

**60 The Black Apple of Gower
(Afal du Brogwyr)** 1952
Signed and dated 'Ceri
Richards '52' lower R.
Inscribed 'AFAL DU
BROGWYR GWROGAETH I
DYLAN THOMAS'
lower centre
Oil on canvas
102 × 76 (40 × 30)
Mrs Rachel Patterson

61 Homage to Beethoven 1953
Signed and dated 'CR 53'
centre R
Oil on canvas

127 × 102 (50 × 40)
*National Museum of Wales,
Cardiff*

**62 Homage to Beethoven
(Beethoven and St
Cecilia)** 1953
Signed and dated lower R
Oil on canvas
114 × 89 (45 × 35)
*Welsh College of Music and
Drama, Cardiff*

PAINTINGS 1950s

**63 Blue Vortex in the
Primaries** 1952–3
Signed and dated 'CR 52 '53'
lower R
Oil on canvas
102 × 127 (40 × 50)
British Council

**64 The Return of the Patient
(The Unconscious
Man)** 1953
Signed and dated 'CR Oct 53'
lower R
Oil on canvas
127 × 102 (50 × 40)
*National Museum of Wales,
Cardiff*

65 Cycle of Nature 1955
Signed and dated 'Ceri
Richards 55' lower R
Oil on canvas
152 × 152 (60 × 60)
Tate Gallery (T83)

66 Cycle of Nature 1955–6
Signed and dated 'Ceri
Richards – 55/56' lower R
Oil on canvas
127 × 127 (50 × 50)
F.E. McWilliam

67 **'Do not go gentle into that good night'** 1956
Signed and dated 'Ceri Richards '56' lower R
Oil on canvas
106.5 × 71 (43 × 28)
Tate Gallery (T439)

68 **Blue Nude** 1957
Signed and dated 'Ceri Richards 1957' lower R
Oil on canvas
101.5 × 152 (40 × 60)
Estate of the artist

69 **The Deposition** 1958
Signed and dated 'Ceri Richards 1958' lower R
Oil on canvas
152 × 182.5 (60 × 72)
Swansea St Mary

LA CATHÉDRALE ENGLOUTIE – Paintings & Constructions 1959–62

70 **La Cathédrale Engloutie (Arabesque 1)** 1959
Signed 'Ceri Richards 1959' on back
Oil on canvas
152 × 152 (60 × 60)
Estate of the artist

71 **La Cathédrale Engloutie I** 1959
Signed and dated 'Ceri Richards 59' lower L
Oil on canvas
152 × 102 (60 × 40)
Private Collection

72 **La Cathédrale Engloutie III** 1960
Signed and dated 'Ceri Richards '60' lower L
Oil on canvas
152 × 152 (60 × 60)
Glynn Vivian Art Gallery & Museum, Swansea

73 **La Cathédrale Engloutie (augmentez progressivement)** 1960–61
Signed and dated
Oil on canvas (triptych)
152 × 456 (60 × 180)
National Museum of Wales, Cardiff

74 **La Cathédrale Engloutie (profondement calme)** 1961
Signed and dated on reverse
Oil on canvas
152 × 152 (60 × 60)
British Council

75 **La Cathédrale Engloutie (jeux de vagues)** 1961
Signed and dated 'CR 61' lower R
Oil on canvas
152 × 152 (60 × 60)
Estate of the artist

76 **La Cathédrale Engloutie (Arabesque 3)** 1961
Inscribed, signed and dated on stretcher 'La Cathédrale Engloutie/Arabesque 3 Ceri Richards 1961'
Oil on canvas
152 × 152 (60 × 60)
Tate Gallery (T802)

77 **La Cathédrale Engloutie (Sunrise 1)** 1962
Signed and dated 'Ceri Richards '62' lower R
Oil and collage on canvas
76 × 76 (30 × 30)
Dale Owen Esq

78 **La Cathédrale Engloutie** Signed and dated 'Ceri Richards 57' bottom R
Oil on canvas
127 × 127 (50 × 50)
Lord Robbins

79 **La Cathédrale Engloutie (sonore sans dureté)** 1962
Signed and dated on back
Oil on canvas
127 × 127 (50 × 50)
British Council

80 **La Cathédrale Engloutie (Blue Swirl)** 1960
Signed and dated 'Ceri Richards 1960' lower R
Relief construction, wood, metal bells, and mixed media on painted wood
30 × 30.4 ($11\frac{3}{4}$ × 12)
Rhiannon Gooding

81 **La Cathédrale Engloutie** 1960
Relief construction, wood, metal, metal bells and collage on painted wood
76 × 76 (30 × 30)
Private Collection

82 **La Cathédrale Engloutie (Gothic Image)** 1962
Relief construction, wood, metal, metal bells and collage on painted wood
60 × 49.5 ($23\frac{1}{2}$ × $19\frac{1}{2}$)
Junior Common Room, St Anne's College, Oxford

83 **La Cathédrale Engloutie (La Belle Chalice)** 1962
Signed and dated 'CERI RICHARDS MARCH 1962' lower R, Inscribed 'Souvenir de la Cathédrale Engloutie de Claude Debussy – La 'Bell'-e Chalice'

Relief construction, wood,
metal, metal bells, collage and
mixed media on wood
48 × 66 (19 × 26)
Estate of the artist

**84 Souvenir de la Cathédrale
Engloutie** 1960–62
Inscribed, signed and dated
'Souvenir pour la Cathédrale
Engloutie de Claude Debussy
Ceri Richards 1960–62'
Relief construction, wood,
metal, metal bells and mixed
media on painted wood
84.5 × 71 (33 × 28)
Estate of the artist

**85 La Cathédrale Engloutie
(profondément calme)** 1962
Signed and dated 'Ceri
Richards 62' Lower L
Oil on canvas
127 × 101.5 (50 × 40)
Private Collection

LATE PAINTINGS 1962–69

**86 'The force that through the
green fuse'** 1965
Signed and dated 'Ceri
Richards '65'
Inscribed 'The force that
through the green fuse drives
the flower drives my green
age Ceri Richards April 1965'
on stretcher
Oil on canvas
127 × 127 (50 × 50)
Estate of the artist

87 Jardins sous la pluie 1967
Signed and dated 'Ceri
Richards 1967' on back
Oil on canvas

127 × 101.5 (50 × 40)
Estate of the artist

88 Jardins sous la pluie 1967
Signed and dated 'Ceri
Richards 1967' on back
Oil on canvas
127 × 127 (50 × 50)
Mr & Mrs Andras Kalman

89 Clair de Lune (Venice)
Signed and dated 'Ceri
Richards 1967' on back
Oil on canvas
127 × 101.5 (50 × 40)
Estate of the Artist

**90 Music of colours – White
Blossom** 1968
Signed and dated 'Ceri
Richards '68' lower R
Oil on canvas
152 × 152 (60 × 60)
*Glynn Vivian Art Gallery &
Museum, Swansea*

**91 Music of colours – White
Blossom (Requiem for a
Poet)** 1968
Signed and dated 'Ceri
Richards 68' lower R
Oil on canvas
127 × 101.5 (50 × 40)
Robert C. Williams

92 Summer 1968
Signed and dated on back
Oil on canvas
127 × 127 (50 × 50)
Government Art Collection

93 The Seasons 1964–69
Signed and dated 'Ceri
Richards 64–69' lower R
Oil on canvas
152 × 152 (60 × 60)
Estate of the artist

94 Harvest 1969
Signed and dated on back
Oil on canvas
101.5 × 127 (40 × 50)
Private Collection

DRAWINGS

I
**'The force that through the green
fuse drives·the flower'** c.1945
Pen, ink, watercolour and chalk
on paper
27 × 39 (10¾ × 15¼)
Mel & Rhiannon Gooding

II
Rhiannon Sleeping 1946
Pencil on paper
17 × 13.2 (6¾ × 5¼)
Mel & Rhiannon Gooding

III
Rhiannon Asleep 1946
Signed and dated 'Ceri Richards
September 1946' lower R
Pencil on paper
33.4 × 50 (13⅛ × 19¾)
Mel & Rhiannon Gooding

IV
The Rape of the Sabines 1947
Signed and dated 'Ceri Richards
'47' lower R
Pen, ink and watercolour on
paper
37.3 × 54.5 (14⅝ × 21½)
Estate of the artist

V
The Sabine Theme 1947
Signed and dated 'Ceri Richards
1947' lower L
Pen, ink and watercolour on
paper
37.8 × 55.2 (14⅞ × 21⅝)
Estate of the artist

VI
**'The force that through the green
fuse drives the flower'** _c._1947–48
Signed 'Ceri Richards' lower R
Pen, ink and watercolour
on paper
38.5 × 55.5 (15⅛ × 27⅞)
Estate of the artist

VII
Rhiannon 1952
Dated 'November 19 '52' lower R
Pencil on paper
38.5 × 29.5 (15 × 11⅝)
Mel & Rhiannon Gooding

VIII
The Artist's Father in Bed 1957
Dated 'July 1957' lower R;
stamped by Studio CR, lower L
Pencil on paper
38.5 × 49 (15⅛ × 19¼)
Estate of the artist

IX
**Portrait of the Artist's Daughter:
Rachel writing** 1957
Signed 'CR', lower L and dated
'August 11 1957' lower R
Pencil on paper
35 × 48 (14 × 19)
Mrs Rachel Patterson

X
Pianist 1959
Signed and dated 'Ceri Richards
1959' lower R
Pen, ink, watercolour and wash
on paper
33 × 49.5 (13 × 19½)
Estate of the artist

XI
Pianist 1968
Signed and dated 'Ceri Richards
1968' lower R
Pen, ink and watercolour
on paper
37 × 54 (14½ × 21¼)
Mel & Rhiannon Gooding

XII
Bust of Beethoven 1968
Signed and dated 'Ceri Richards
'68' lower R
Pen and ink, watercolour and
gouache on paper
34 × 49.5 (13⅜ × 19½)
Estate of the artist

XIII
The Rape of Europa 1970
Signed and dated 'Ceri Richards
1970' lower R
Pen, ink and watercolour
on paper
56.5 × 76.7 (22¼ × 30¼)
Mel & Rhiannon Gooding

XIV
Two Musicians 1970
Signed and dated 'Ceri Richards
January 1970' lower R
Pen, ink and watercolour
on paper
38 × 56.8 (15 × 22⅜)
Estate of the artist

XV
Tinplate Workers 1942 (?)
Pen and ink, crayon and chalk
on paper
53 × 66 (21 × 26)
Mrs Esther Thomas

XVI
**Tinplate Workers, with
Furnaceman mopping his
brow** 1942
Signed and dated 'Ceri Richards
1942' lower R
Pen and ink, crayon and gouache
on paper
53.5 × 71.8 (21 × 28¼)
Private Collection

XVII
**Five studies for lithographs on
Dylan Thomas themes** 1945
Each signed and dated and the
whole frame inscribed, signed and
dated 'Drawings for the poem by
Dylan Thomas – Ceri Richards
1945' lower R
Ink, chalk and watercolour
on paper
From left to right starting at top
28 × 20.5 (11 × 8), 28.5 × 21
(11¼ × 8¼), 24.7 × 40.5
(9¾ × 16), 28.5 × 20.5 (11¼ × 8),
22.7 × 17 (8¾ × 6¾)
Sir John Rothenstein

XVIII
Prometheus 1970
Signed and dated 'Ceri Richards
'70'
Pen, ink and watercolour
on paper
45.5 × 68.5 (18 × 27)
Private Collection

XIX
The Artist's Father 1942
Pencil on paper
27.5 × 37 (10¾ × 14½)
_National Museum of Wales,
Cardiff_

One-Man Exhibitions

1930–1
Glynn Vivian Art Gallery, Swansea

1942
Leger Gallery, London

1943
National Museum of Wales, Cardiff –
exhibition of worker drawings

1944/6/8 1950/1/3/4/6/7
Redfern Gallery, London

1954
Glynn Vivian Art Gallery, Swansea,
Homage to Two Poets
Retrospective exhibition arranged by
King's College, Durham University,
for a tour of five north country cities

1959
Bear Lane Gallery, Oxford

1960
Whitechapel Gallery, London –
retrospective exhibition
Royal National Eisteddfod of Wales,
Cardiff

1962–3
British Pavilion, XXXI Venice Biennale
– retrospective exhibition and tour to:
Madrid, Barcelona, Brussels, Munich,
Berlin, Delft, Paris

1963
Marlborough New London Gallery

1964
Glynn Vivian Art Gallery, Swansea –
retrospective exhibition

1965
Arnolfini Gallery, Bristol
Marlborough New London Gallery –
retrospective exhibition

1967
Aldeburgh Festival
Kunstnernes Hus, Oslo

1969
Castle Museum, Norwich
Galleria M'Arte, Milan

1970
Gallery Wolfensberger, Zurich
Marlborough Fine Art, London
Einaudi Gallery, Milan

1972
Aldeburgh Festival
Third British International Print
Biennale, Bradford
Fischer Fine Art, London – *Homage to
Ceri Richards 1903–1971*

1973
Contemporary Art Society for Wales
National Museum of Wales, Cardiff –
Memorial Exhibition

1974
Fischer Fine Art, London – relief
constructions, paintings and
drawings, 1931–9
Galleria Cavour, Milan

1975
Patrick Seale Gallery, London
Cambridge Poetry Festival
Edinburgh International Festival –
Royal Scottish Academy

1978
Bruton Gallery, Bruton, Somerset
The Arts Centre, Christ's Hospital,
Horsham

1979
Kettle's Yard, Cambridge

1979/80/81
Graphics exhibition sponsored by
National Museum of Wales and
Southern Arts Association on tour.
(1981 National Museum of Wales,
Curwen Gallery, London)

1981
Warwick Arts Trust – retrospective
exhibition of drawings 1926–71

Selected Group Exhibitions

1934
Zwemmer Gallery – *Objective Abstractions*

1936–7
London Gallery – *The Surrealist Group*

1934
London Gallery – *Living Art in England*

1942
London Museum – *New Movements in Contemporary Art*

1945
Buchholz Gallery, New York – *Six Contemporary British Artists*

1946
Modern British Paintings from the Tate Gallery, exhibition touring Europe

1951
Festival of Britain Exhibition, London – *Sixty Paintings for '51*

1953
Pittsburgh International Exhibition, Carnegie Institute, Pittsburgh
Second Biennale Exhibition, Museu de Arte Moderne, São Paulo

1954
3rd International Exhibition of Prints, Lugano
Venice Biennale
Whitechapel Art Gallery, London – *British Painting and Sculpture*

1955
Pittsburgh International Exhibition, Carnegie Institute, Pittsburgh

1959
Whitechapel Art Gallery *The Graven Image*

1960
Pushkin Museum, Moscow – *British Painting 1920–1960*, and at the Hermitage, Leningrad

1961
Museum of Modern Art, New York – *Art of Assemblage*
Museum of Contemporary Arts, Dallas

1961–2
Pittsburgh International Exhibition, Carnegie Institute, Pittsburgh

1962
Kompass II, Eindhoven

1962–3
San Francisco Museum of Art – *British Art Today*, and tour to: Dallas Museum of Contemporary Arts
Santa Barbara Museum of Art

1963
Dunn International Exhibition, Beaverbrook Art Gallery, Fredericton, Canada, and Tate Gallery, London

1964
Tate Gallery, London – *54–64 Painting and Sculpture of a Decade*
Bochum – *Profil III – Englische Kunst der Gegenwart*
XXXII Venice Biennale
Pittsburgh International Exhibition, Carnegie Institute, Pittsburgh

1965
Marlborough Fine Art, London – *Art in Britain 1930–40*

1966
Marlborough New London Gallery, with Sydney Nolan and John Piper

1967
Tate Gallery, London – *Recent British Painting* (The Peter Stuyvesant Foundation Collection)

1968
Kunstverein Hamburg – *Britische Kunst Heute*

1971
Hamet Gallery – *Britain's Contribution to Surrealism of the 30s and 40s*

1973/4
Camden Arts Centre – *Lithographs from the Curwen Studio: a retrospective of fifteen years of printmaking*

1974
Scottish Arts Council, Edinburgh – *Art Then*

1977
Tate Gallery, London – *Artists at Curwen*

1978
Hayward Gallery, London *Dada & Surrealism Reviewed*

1979
Hayward Gallery, London – *Thirties*

Select Bibliography

1930
HUBERT WELLINGTON Foreword in the catalogue of the exhibition at Glynn Vivian Art Gallery, Swansea

1933
JOHN PIPER 'Contemporary English Drawing', *The Listener* (11 October)

1934
CERI RICHARDS Answers to questions in the catalogue of the *Objective Abstractions* exhibition, Zwemmer Gallery (March–April) (Reprinted in *Sanesi*, 1976)

1944
H. S. WILLIAMSON 'Ceri Richards', *Horizon* (April)

1950
ERIC NEWTON *In My View* (Longmans)
MARY SORRELL 'Portrait of the Artist', *Art News and Review* (29 July)

1951
PATRICK HERON 'Round the London Art Galleries', *The Listener* (13 September)

1953
JOHN BERGER 'Ceri Richards at the Redfern', *New Statesman and Nation* (14 May)

1954
COLIN ANDERSON Foreword in the catalogue of the retrospective exhibition organised by King's College, University of Durham

1956
JOHN BERGER 'Ceri Richards', *New Statesman and Nation* (14 April)

1958
TOM PHILLIPS 'St Edmund Hall altarpiece', *The Oxford Magazine* (4 December)

1959
HERBERT READ *Art Since 1945* (Thames & Hudson)

1960
JOHN BERGER *Permanent Red* (Methuen)
DAVID THOMPSON Introduction in the catalogue of the retrospective exhibition, Whitechapel Art Gallery 'A painter's poetic vision', *The Times* (30 June)
ALAN BOWNESS 'Metaphor in Paint', *Observer* (3 July)
JOHN RUSSELL 'The Season's Climax', *Sunday Times* (3 July)

1961
ALAN BOWNESS 'The Content of Contemporary British Painting', *The London Magazine* (July)
J.R. WEBSTER Introduction of the monograph published by the Welsh Committee of the Arts Council of Great Britain on the occasion of the Eisteddfod Exhibition

1962
JOHN ROTHENSTEIN *British Art Since 1900* (Phaidon)
JOHN RUSSELL Introduction to the catalogue of the retrospective exhibition, British Pavilion, XXXI Venice Biennale
ROBERTO SANESI 'Gli Stranieri alla Biennale', *Le Arti* No.6 (Milan, June)

1963
MERVYN LEVY 'The Celtic Eye of Ceri Richards', *Studio* (July)
DAVID THOMPSON *Ceri Richards*, Art in Progress series (Methuen)
MICHAEL LEVEY 'Around the Galleries', *London Magazine* (September)

1964
NOEL BARBER *Conversations with Painters* (Collins)
ALAN BOWNESS 'Music and Colour in the Painting of Ceri Richards', *Motif* No.12
VERNON WATKINS Introduction to the retrospective exhibition at the Glynn Vivian Art Gallery, Swansea 'Exuberance', *Viewpoint* No.1

1965
ROBERT MELVILLE Introduction to the catalogue of the retrospective at the Marlborough New London Gallery

1966
ROBERTO SANESI 'Note per Ceri Richards, simbolista elementare', *Essere* No.2 (Milan)

1967
CERI RICHARDS 'Looking at Picasso's Sculptures', *Studio International* (July/August)

1968
FREDERICK GIBBERD *Metropolitan Cathedral of Christ the King, Liverpool* (Architectural Press)

1970
JOHN ROTHENSTEIN *Time's Thievish Progress* (Cassell)

1970
CERI RICHARDS 'Remembering
Vernon' in *Vernon Watkins
1906–1967* (Faber & Faber)
BRYAN ROBERTSON 'Ceri's Celtic
Clarity', *The Spectator* (10 October)

1971
ROBERTO SANESI 'Il re della metafora',
Corriere della Sera (Milan,
15 November)

1972
JOHN RUSSELL, FRANCES RICHARDS and
others, Introduction to *Homage to Ceri
Richards 1903–1971*, catalogue of
the exhibition at Fischer Fine Art Ltd,
London
JOHN ORMOND 'Ceri Richards Root and
Branch', *Planet* 10 (February/March)

1973
ROBERTO SANESI *The Graphic Works of
Ceri Richards* (Cerastico Editore,
Milan. Distributed in UK by Martin,
Brian & O'Keeffe)

1973
JOHN ORMOND Introduction to the
catalogue of the Memorial Exhibition,
National Museum of Wales, Cardiff
GIANCARLO VIGORELLI 'Ceri Richards e
Roberto Sanesi: Un incontro' in the
prospectus booklet for *Journey Toward
the North* (Cerastico, Milan)

1974
JOHN ROTHENSTEIN *Modern English
Painters* (Macdonald)
JOHN RUSSELL Introduction to the
catalogue of the exhibition of relief
constructions, paintings and
drawings 1931–1939, at Fischer Fine
Art Ltd, London

1975
ALAN BOWNESS Introduction to the
catalogue of the retrospective
exhibition at Royal Scottish Academy,
Edinburgh

1976
ROBERTO SANESI *Ceri Richards, Rilievi,
disegni e dipinti 1931/1940* (La Nuova
Foglio Editrice, Milan)
JOHN SUNDERLAND *Painting in Britain
1525 to 1975* (Phaidon)

1977
PAT GILMOUR *Artists at Curwen*
(Tate Gallery)

1978
MEL GOODING Introduction to an
exhibition of the Debussy paintings at
The Arts Centre, Christ's Hospital,
Horsham

1979
MEL GOODING *Ceri Richards Graphics*
(National Museum of Wales)

1980
MICHAEL JACOBS and MALCOLM
WARNER *The Phaidon Companion to Art
and Artists in the British Isles*
(Phaidon)
CERI RICHARDS *Drawings to Poems by
Dylan Thomas* Introduction by
Richard Burns (The Enitharmon
Press)

List of Lenders

Artist's Estate 44, 68, 70,75, 83, 84, 86, 87, 89, 93, IV–VI, VIII, X, XII, XIV

Arts Council of Great Britian 37, 46

Bassetlaw District Council 49
British Council 63, 74, 79

Fisher Fine Art, London 9

Arthur Giardelli 52
Mr and Mrs Wilfred Giardelli 47, 50
Glynn Vivian Art Gallery & Museum 3, 18, 38, 72, 90
Mel & Rhiannon Gooding 56, 58, 80, I–III, VII, XI, XIII

Government Art Collection 92

Mr and Mrs Andras Kalman 88

Manchester City Art Galleries 10
F.E. McWilliam 35, 66

National Museum of Wales 5, 36, 39, 61, 64, 73, XIX

Dale Owen 77

Mrs Rachel Patterson 43, 57, 59, 60, IX

Portsmouth City Museum and Art Gallery 1

Private Collections 2, 41, 42,53, 71, 81, 85, 94, XVI, XVIII

Frances Richards 4, 6, 11–14, 16, 17, 19–26, 29–33, 45
Lord Robbins 78
Mr and Mrs Eugene Rosenberg 40
Sir John Rothenstein XVII

St Anne's College, Oxford 82
Swansea St Mary 69

Tate Gallery 7, 8, 15, 27, 28, 34, 54, 65, 67, 76
Mrs Esther Thomas XV

University College of Wales 48, 51

Walker Art Gallery 55
Welsh College of Music and Drama 62
Robert C. Williams 91

Acknowledgments

We are grateful to J. M. Dent & Sons Ltd and to the Trustees for the copyright for the late Dylan Thomas for permission to quote *The Force that Through the Green Fuse* (p.19) and to Faber & Faber and Mrs Gwen Watkins for permission to quote *Music of Colours – White Blossom* by Vernon Watkins (pp.20–1) in the introduction to this catalogue.